The New
Devil's Dictionary

By ED KONSTANT

ISBN 978-1-4303-2657-1

Published by Lulu
Printed in the United States of America

For Barbara

Foreword

For more than a century, Ambrose Bierce has been the patron saint of cynics. The path toward his destiny began with wicked definitions of words of the time that appeared in his newspaper columns in various cities of the United States. Canonization took place when these definitions were collected in a volume published in 1906 as "The Devil's Dictionary," which had been changed from his original title of "The Cynic's Word Book" in order to make it more marketable. Full sainthood was achieved when Bierce went to take a look at the Mexican Revolution in 1913 and vanished from public sight, a mystery that never has been solved.

Like all saints, Ambrose Bierce lived in an earlier time when words meant different things than they would generations later. Thus, this book. Not only have new definitions been given to old words (only a relative handful of words defined by Bierce have been redefined in this book), many new words that did not exist in Bierce's time have since come into common usage due to the changes that have affected society since the publication of his original work.

Was Ambrose Bierce a true cynic? Or a satirist? Or a combination of both? And, what is a cynic, anyway? I like to think I found the answer to that question a few years ago one summer morning in Dieppe, France, where my wife Barbara and I were sipping coffee after just finishing a late breakfast at a sidewalk table outside the Café Suisse. We were deciding how to spend the rest of the day when a man and woman sat at the table next to ours. Because they were speaking English, rarely heard in Dieppe, Barbara opened a conversation with them, an American man and a French woman, both in their mid to late thirties. They were en route from their home in Paris to London, via the English Channel ferry that connected Dieppe to, England.. When he told us that he wrote screenplays, Barbara remarked on the coincidence of our meeting.

"My husband is a writer, too," she said.

The screenwriter turned toward me and asked:

"What kind of writing do you do?"

"Fiction," I replied.

"What kind of fiction?"

"News."

"That's good," he said with a laugh. "I like that."

Barbara smiled and continued the subject with the remark:

"My husband's a cynic."

The screenwriter's reply was perfect:

"You mean he's a realist."

A

Abattoir: A French word for "slaughterhouse," which has found increasingly widespread use in the United States because Americans do not want to know how the beef, pork and poultry they buy has made its way to their dining tables.

Abandonment: Action expected by a colleague when you are facing a crisis.

Abscond: The last act of a financial consultant entrusted with your money.

Absurdity: Public behavior of others that helps keep the thinking person sane.

Abuse: Something people do simply because they can.

Accident: The unforeseen result of someone's mistake.

Accommodate: What people do for others while searching for an elusive alternative.

Accordion: A musical instrument that should be played only by the French.

Accountant: A person whose skill with numbers can deceive investors into believing that a company's losses are actually profits.

Accuracy: A lesson taught in journalism school to students who are quick to unlearn once they are employed as journalists.

Ace: A card that every good negotiator has up his sleeve.

Acknowledgment: Something just short of an acceptance of another person or someone else's idea, usually tendered grudgingly.

Acolyte: Once a title of honor for boys during Catholic religious services, now something that they should at least think about twice before accepting a priest's invitation to become one.

Actor: Someone who listens only when others are talking about him.

Additive: A concoction that seems to be most frequently used for ingestion by a person's digestive system or a motor vehicle engine.

Adjective: The most annoying form of descriptive word in the English language, especially when used by advertising copywriters.

Admission: A partial truth spoken by someone in an effort to explain why he or she did something foolish.

Admonition: Criticism accompanied by a lecture.

Adventure: An undertaking that usually makes its participants wish they had stayed at home.

Adventurer: One of many Europeans of generations ago who believed that the grass grew greener on the other side of the fence in the Americas.

Advertisement: A printed or broadcast announcement designed to convince people to spend money on a product or service that rarely delivers what it promises.

Advice: Something that should be ignored.

Adult: A condition that can be cured only by death.

Aerobics: A silly form of exercise that women pay to perform in the company of other women rather than do it in the privacy of their own homes.

Affidavit: One or more pages of written half-truths that people involved in legal proceedings prefer rather than be asked to swear in front of a judge that they will tell "the whole truth and nothing but the truth" when they have no intention of doing so.

Aficionado: Something people call themselves in the belief that others will see them as experts in a subject of which they know little.

Age: Something that wishes it had not misspent youth.

Agnostic: A wannabee atheist who is hedging his or her bet.

Airhead: A person, usually under thirty years of age, whose favorite word is "awesome."

Airport: A place filled with every irritation except opera singing.

Alarm: Designed to alert the public of possible danger, it has become an infernal device designed to rob people of sleep.

Alchemist: Someone employed by a pharmaceutical company to develop new so-called medications.

Alcohol: An ingredient of a beverage consumed in record proportions in Washington, D.C., especially by politicians and journalists.

Alibi: An excuse intended to support a guilty person's claim of innocence, pending the accused's ability to convince a friend or relative to lie in court.

Alien: When followed by the word "illegal," a person who is willing to work.

Alleged: A word being used with increased frequency by the news media in an effort to protect themselves from legal action after they have maligned someone in a hasty effort to report the news first without thoroughly checking the facts.

Allergies: God's practical jokes.

Ally: A questionable friend.

Aloof: The attitude displayed by a person who has difficulty mixing with other people.

Amateur: A person who will do something for nothing that someone else will do only for money.

Ambassador: Someone sent to a foreign country to lie on behalf of his or her government.

Ambience: A pretentious word used to describe the atmosphere of a restaurant or hotel room, thereby allowing the management to add to the cost of services.

Amendment: An attachment to proposed defective legislation that is all but guaranteed to make it even worse.

Ambush: Treachery to the people who are attacked, good strategy to the attackers.

America: A place where parents obey their children.

Ancestor: A long-dead relative who is either praised for his or her accomplishments or whose family connections never are mentioned because of a shady past.

Ancient: Anything at least 1,000 years old to a historian, 100 years old to the rest of the adult population and 10 years old to anyone under the age of 18.

Anchovy: Marinated fish used mostly to spoil the taste of pizza.

Annexation: A process by which people seek to incorporate others into their group, usually against the will of the latter.

Anonymity: A hiding place for people who are unwilling to take the credit or blame for controversy.

Antiques: Junk pretending to have value because of its age.

Apathy: The normal condition of most eligible voters living in a democracy.

Apocalypse: The day of the end of the world and final judgment as announced by fringe religions that, when it fails to arrive, are quick to acknowledge their miscalculation and then set another calendar date.

Apology: Demanded from anyone deemed guilty of a severe mistake, never given publicly by politicians, rarely given by women and, when given by men usually leaves them feeling more badly than they did before.

Appeasement: A betrayal of principals in international affairs.

Appetite: Something that should be subdued by anyone who does not appreciate fine food.

Apple: A fruit that once, ate daily, was believed to keep people healthy, but now more recognized as a computer, whose daily use will eventually require medical or psychiatric treatment.

Aquarium: A watery prison for fish.

Arbitration: A system used to override deadlocked negotiations in which both sides agree to abide by the decision of an arbiter, who usually produces a settlement that results in one party getting more than it was willing to settle for at the expense of the other.

Architecture: Once a highly praised art that has degenerated into a popular form of modern design used in the construction of buildings at the cheapest possible cost.

Architecture: Once a highly praised art that has degenerated into a popular form of modern design used in the construction of buildings at the cheapest possible cost.

Arrival: The scheduled time that is rarely met by an airline that has promised its paying passengers that it will deliver them to a destination.

Arson: The businessman's escape from bankruptcy.

Artist: A person of dubious talent whose death is eagerly awaited by collectors who have purchased his works.

Artsy: Suspect and pretentious design or behavior, usually followed by the word "fartsy."

Asiatic: A word resented by people who live in Asia because it usually is followed by the word "hordes."

Ass: Someone other than yourself.

Assurance: Something which, when given, should be doubted.

Astrologer: A con artist.

Asylum: A place where elected lawmakers meet to design rules that determine how the rest of the citizenry should live.

Athlete: Someone who purchases drugs to reduce pain or enhance performance in a sport so that he or she can perform at a professional level in order to make enough money to acquire more such drugs to be able to earn the maximum amount of money that will be needed after retirement to purchase even more drugs to ease the pains and other ailments resulting from having been a professional athlete.

Atmosphere: The dumping ground for invisible toxic waste generated by private industry and the public.

Attic: Storage space for unwanted junk that people refuse to throw away.

Audition: The end of a career for most persons hoping to become show business stars.

Australia: A country where economic and social development has been stunted by the inability of geographers to agree on whether it is a continent or an island.

Audience: The necessary evil on opening night of a stage play.

Authentic: A word used to sell anything not worth the price.

Authority: Something that always should be distrusted.

Authorization: An action that a junior government official never should expect to receive from a senior when asked to perform a covert task.

Autobiography: An exaggerated memoir of the author's life, with an emphasis on positive accomplishments that never quite occurred the way he or she describes them.

Automobile: A mechanical device that can cause people to lose the use of their feet.

Autopsy: A post-mortem medical procedure once hailed for its value in solving crimes and protecting the public from epidemics, it has more commonly become simply a desecration of the dead.

Available: What is left of what once were greater choices.

Avarice: One of the Seven Deadly Sins that has evolved over time into a virtue.

Award: A trophy, medal or ribbon that once was given to people as a prize for excellence in achievement, but now often rewards those who lose or simply participate.

Awesome: A secret code word used by airheads to identify themselves to each other.

B

Babble: A language spoken whenever members of the United States Senate or House of Representatives manage to make one of their infrequent appearances on the floors of their respective chambers of Congress..

Baboon: One of the many members of the family of apes whose antics often resemble those of elected public officials at work.

Bachelor: A happy man.

Bacon: Much desired in Europe as an accompaniment to eggs at breakfast because of its lean qualities and equally desired in the United States because of its high fat content.

Badge: Once a symbol of heraldic honor in medieval times, it has evolved into something anyone can wear if he or she pays the dues required to join a club.

Baggage: Something everyone tries to keep out of site when entering a relationship with someone of the opposite sex.

Bail: A large amount of money paid to a court of law by an accused to temporarily stay out of jail while awaiting trial, thus giving him or her the option of fleeing to avoid conviction.

Baker: An artisan in a field that has all but vanished in the United States thanks to the American public's fondness for chemical ingredients.

Balance: Something that banks unreasonably ask customers to do with their checking accounts.

Ballot: An election day device designed to confuse voters.

Bandit: A romanticized criminal profession practiced in past centuries by legendary figures, now called common thieves.

Banjo: A musical instrument played mostly by people with twelve fingers and large round heads.

Bank: An institution founded by burglars, who prefer to operate legally.

Bankruptcy: The "American way" out of debt, as described by President Ronald Reagan.

Baptism: A religious ritual during which innocent infants are subjected to unwanted abuse that supposedly cleanses them of sins they are too young to have committed.

Bar: Also known as a tavern or pub, a place where people drive to, park their motor vehicles in a space provided for that purpose by the owner of the bar, then drive home after being served and drinking alcoholic beverages beyond the limit allowed by law for driving.

Barbarian: Someone who can change society for the better.

Barbecue: A device that allows men to pretend that they know how to cook.

Bargain: Something that proves the adage that "you get what you pay for."

Baseball: A sport where failure is used to measure success. For example, a batter who fails to register a base hit during two out of three plate appearances is crowned as a superstar, and a team that loses more than 70 games during a season can qualify as the national champion.

Basketball: A circus of giants, with points.

Bathroom: An American euphemism for a room, which may not have a bath, that is used mostly for bodily functions that Americans often pretend do not occur.

Battle: A violent event that allows military officers of one side to make enough mistakes that result in the deaths of more of their soldiers than those of the other side, generally leading to more such events until the side that makes fewer mistakes wins the war.

Beach: Bordering the waters of the sea, a strip of sandy shore used by the entertainment industry to produce third-rate movies and television shows featuring attractive, scantily clad, brainless young men and women armed with volleyballs and surfboards.

Beard: A natural disguise for hiding personality defects.

Beast: Creatures that prove that the adage "survival of the least fit."

Beatitude: A riddle.

Beatnik: An early version of the 1960's Hippie, with the added pretension of cultural awareness.

Beauty: A natural condition people seek to improve, usually with bad results.

Because: When uttered during a disagreement, a word introducing an excuse.

Bed: A place where people should be allowed to remain undisturbed at least until sometime in the early afternoon.

Bedlam: Spectator sport.

Beef: The flesh of cow's corpse.

Beer: A beverage for boys.

Beggar: An honest thief.

Behalf: When used between the words "on" and "of," something that someone is claiming to be doing for another, while really doing it for selfish reasons.

Belief: The opposite of logic.

Benefits: Something that employers offer to their workers because higher wages would be more costly to pay.

Benevolent: A word used by dictators to justify their rule.

Beret: A silly hat that should be worn only by artists.

Berliner: What President John F. Kennedy called himself in an attempt to express his solidarity with the tens of thousands of people gathered to hear him speak on the western side of the infamous Berlin Wall in the nineteen-sixties, being as unaware as his speech writers that the phrase he had shouted to the crowd and the television cameras meant "I am a doughnut."

Betrayal: Something allies eventually do to each other.

Bewildered: The human race.

Bible: A religious book in which God often is portrayed as the villain.

Bigamist: Someone in two unhappy marriages.

Bilingual: A person who usually is not an American.

Bills: Debts to be paid when you run out of excuses for avoiding them.

Biography: A dull account of the life of a good person or a fascinating account of the life of a rogue.

Birth: The first step on the path to death.

Bland: Meals prepared by mother.

Blasphemy: The thinking man's prayer.

Bonus: A disgracefully excessive amount of money given to a corporate executive for doing the job for which he or she already is overpaid, all at the expense of the company investors and its underpaid workers.

Books: The ultimate in furniture.

Bore: Someone whose conversation is limited to one subject that no one else cares about.

Bourbon: Distilled spirits posing as whiskey.

Boulevard: A wide street designed without thought for pedestrian safety.

Bowling: A game, sometimes referred to as a "sport," in which the main qualification for participants seems to be an ability to drink beer.

Boxing: The purest of athletic competition.

Boycott: A ridiculous and ineffective method of attempting to pressure corporations and even nations into changing their behavior.

Brain: The body's most important organ, yet oddly, about only five percent of it is used by its human hosts.

Brake: A foot pedal on a motor vehicle, usually ignored by most motorists until the last possible moment of application.

Brandy: A French pretender to the throne occupied by single malt Scotch.

Brassiere: The only guaranteed means of support for a poor woman.

Bread: One of the earliest known food staples, which Americans have forgotten to appreciate.

Breakfast: The most important meal of the day, except in America.

Breeze: Something that disappears from Florida during the hottest months of the year.

Bribe: Extra income for public officials.

Broker: A lengthened version of the word "broke," which is the condition a person is left in after taking poor advice from someone claiming to be an expert in financial investments.

Brothel: An indoor amusement park for men.

Bubbly: An affliction peculiar to some women, who should be quarantined so as not to spread the contagion to others.

Bucs: One of a silly series of professional sports teams nicknames shortened by lazy sports editors because the name "Buccaneers" was too long to fit into the headlines of newspapers in the Tampa Bay area of Florida..

Buffet: A table filled with a variety of dishes pretending to be a gourmet feast, but really an excuse for people who lie about their weight to eat too much.

Bulge: Something guaranteed to form around the waist of someone who has attended too many buffets or drunk too much beer.

Bullets: Small metal objects, some of which are destined to end up imbedded in the flesh of a person.

Bureau: The title of a government office that should be viewed with suspicion.

Bureaucracy: A place where you can find anything that will not be done.

Bureaucrat: A public leech.

Butcher: Another name for a surgeon.

Butterfly: A noble winged insect so admired by people for its beauty by people who express their appreciation for the unfortunate creature by capturing it, then skewering it with a sharp pin onto a board for display.

Byte: Once the smallest unit of a computer program, but as the result of technological evolution it has grown in size, first to thousands, then millions, then billions, to the confusion of all but the most computer literate.

C

Cabbage: A vegetable so maligned that when the word "head" is attached to it at the end, it refers to someone classified as an idiot.

Caber: A wooden telephone pole that men in Scotland attempt to toss for distance in what has become the annual backbreaking competition of festive Scottish clan games.

Cackle: When heard during a meeting of two or more persons, at least one of the listeners should beware.

Cacophony: An unpleasant mixing of sounds, sometimes intended to inflict psychological pain on the listener, as in rock n' roll music.

Cad: Something that most men become at one time or another.

Cadet: A young person who is being trained, under the guise of an education, to learn the military arts, including how to aim and fire a deadly weapon at another person.

California: A state set aside by the United States as a refuge for displaced alien refugees from outer space.

Cambridge: A dull version of Oxford.

Camera: A device that takes photographs intended to be worth 1,000 words, when in reality one word generally is sufficient to sum up the result.

Campaign: A traveling political circus in which the star performers are clowns.

Camping: An outdoor vacation experience with the discomforts of life.

Canary: The most common species of birds that their caring human owners keep imprisoned for life.

Candidate: Someone unfit for political office.

Candor: Something that people ask of others, only to regret receiving it.

Cant: Sanctimony in the form of a sermon.

Cantankerous: A skill acquired with age.

Capable: The description of someone who falls short of expectations.

Capsize: The fate of passenger ferries launched from Third World ports.

Carafe: A vessel in which mediocre wine is served.

Career: The destroyer of family life.

Caricature: A cartoon drawn by an artist whose eyes see the real us.

Cartel: An organization of corporations that maximizes profits through price-gouging despite the public admonishment of governments, which secretly look the other way because they lack the courage to take on the powerful wealthy.

Casino: A bank that takes money from the public without paying a return.

Cassock: The uniform of a pedophile.

Cat: A domestic pet that, once it becomes comfortable in your home, tolerates your presence there.

Catalogue: A wish book of merchandise that delivers disappointment to the door of customers..

Catholicism: The largest branch of the Christian faith, whose popularity is based on its policy of allowing its followers to lead lives of sin while promising them an afterlife of salvation as long as they seek forgiveness before death.

Cavalry: Horse soldiers that made war worth watching.

Celebrity: Someone who has gained fame by engaging in notorious acts, which eventually will lead to a loss of popularity.

Celibacy: The best reason for avoiding a career as a priest.

Cellphone: A public annoyance that only some restaurateurs in Italy have been able to control by requiring patrons to check the offending devices at the front door before being seated.

Censorship: A battle cry used by writers and other artists when their employers make decisions with which they do not agree.

Censure: Something that should be applied to every elected official at least once during their careers.

Census: An ineffective government attempt to count the numbers of people living within the borders of its nation; the last true census was that of the 11th Century English Domesday Book.

Centrist: A politician whose only conviction is to refuse to take stands on controversial issues in an effort to earn more votes than other candidates.

Challenged: The latest in a series of words used by the government in its unending public pacification effort, in this case directed at persons who suffer from physical problems. "Challenged" has been preceded, in reverse order, by "disadvantaged," "disabled," "handicapped" and "crippled."

Chance: The only thing guaranteed in life.

Chaos: World events, as evidenced by the nightly television news.

Character: The human expression of flawed.

Charisma: The first requisite of a candidate for election to political office, regardless of his or her lack of ability in other areas.

Charity: An organization that collects money for the poor, then distributes it only after taking a large percentage off the top for its directors.

Charlatan: A public speaker.

Chastity: A virtue long held in disrepute.

Cheap: A once acceptable word that has been swept under the linguistic rug in the United States and replaced by poor substitutes such as "discount."

Cheerleading: A sex show on the sidelines of sports events which, when the event becomes dull, gets most of the attention of male spectators.

Cheer: A sound designed to instill pride in the winners, with no regard for the feelings of the losers.

Cheerful: An unnatural condition, experienced almost exclusively by people who do not read newspapers or watch televised news.

Cheese: A food that should be limited in variety lest it make it impossible to rule, according to Charles de Gaulle, who claimed that no one could govern France because it produced 246 different types of cheese.

Chic: Anything considered fashionable by the pretentious.

Children: Offspring who are a joy to their parents until they reach 13 years old.

Chivalry: A concept bemoaned by romanticists who mourn its disappearance from society because of a belief that it was a gentle way of life in a gentler time; in actuality it was anything but, as evidenced by historical accounts of the Middle Ages.

Choice: A right granted to people by the Lord, but denied to them by organized religion.

Chopsticks: An inefficient Chinese eating device used in the Western world by men and women seeking to impress each other with what they believe is cultural sophistication.

Chorus: The sounds of displeasure arising from a crowd that disagrees with a decision, usually related to athletics.

Christian: Someone who practices what he dare not preach.

Christmas: A commercial orgy in the guise of a sacred holiday.

Chronicle: A carefully detailed record of half-truths.

Chuckle: Mild laughter sounded by someone pretending to understand the humor of others.

Church: A place of worship built at enormous cost with the help of donations from parishioners whose resulting impoverishment is later ignored by the people who took their contributions.

Circumcision: Barbaric surgery performed on a defenseless male infants by adults who would never consent to it for themselves had they already not been circumcised.

Circus: Any large gathering of people to hear a politician or preacher talk.

Civilization: A failed experiment.

Classic: Once used to describe literature, music and other art forms that have stood the test of decades of time, now relegated by marketers to the role of supporting inferior productions and performances of recent vintage.

Clay: A material of which the feet of the leaders of great nations has been molded.

Cleric: Someone who lacks the skills to gain employment in the world beyond religion.

Clever: A natural talent of a relatively small number of people who are able to get on in life without much effort, but who also eventually cannot resist pushing their luck too far.

Cliche: Words of wisdom that are repeated too often.

Client: A customer who is overcharged for a service.

Clock: A device designed to remind us where to go where we do not want or do what is not necessary.

Closet: A metaphorical place where people hide their dirty little secrets.

Coalition: A shaky alliance.

Cockroach: Believed by many experts to be the oldest surviving creature on Earth, it also is considered by some of them to be the most likely living thing to inherit the planet.

Collapse: The fate of every human society.

College: An expensive baby-sitting service.

Colony: Foreign land ruthlessly seized by unscrupulous adventurers, usually with the support of their governments.

Commander: The leader of an organization or nation en route to disaster.

Commandments: Originally a list of 10 sacred biblical laws presumably given by God to Moses, who brought them down from the heights of a mountain; over the centuries they have been expanded to dozens as people found that having only 10 to break was too restrictive.

Commerce: The part of the system of global economics that allows business to legally cheat consumers.

Committee: A group of persons appointed to study a problem and produce a report that spends the rest of its days filling space on a shelf.

Communism: A political system intended to grant equality to all people, while quietly granting special privileges to its leaders.

Comparison: A technique used to convince the public of the superiority of one thing, or even one group of people, of superiority over another.

Compatibility: An elusive goal for two people about to begin a relationship.

Complaint: The true test of the maxim that the "customer is always right."

Completely: One of the most misused words in the English language, especially by newscasters, who use it unnecessarily when describing disasters (as in "completely destroyed" or "completely cured"). Something simply either is destroyed or it is not, cured or is not. etc.

Complex: The description of a problem that people fail to solve because of their impatience.

Compromise: An outcome sought by nations willing to sacrifice their principles, but ignored by those which are arrogant.

Conclusion: The end of a flawed exercise in research.

Conference: An opportunity for government officials, industry executives, educators and other so-called experts to discuss new ways to avoid meaningful work.

Confession: A half-truth.

Conformity: A 21st Century plague.

Congress: A group of 535 persons who, instead of representing the American voters who elected them to public office, find that they are able to amass power and wealth by representing special interests such as corporations and labor unions.

Conscience: Something with which successful people can live.

Consensus: The majority one day, the minority the next.

Conservation: Profanity uttered at a meeting of directors of an oil corporation.

Conservative: Someone who believes that less government is better until they acquire the means to increase it.

Consideration: What governments proclaim they will give to proposals that, in fact, are dead on arrival.

Consolation: An optimist's alternative to self-pity.

Constitution: A document hailed by governments as a sacred guarantee of the observation of law and citizen rights, only to be overlooked by national leaders when it suits their purposes.

Consumer: A woman.

Contempt: A talent that requires considerable introspection.

Contract: An agreement between two parties written in favor of the one who has the best lawyer.

Convention: Audience participation at a comedy performance.

Convict: A lifetime profession for most people tried for crimes, despite the best intentions of social reformers.

Cookie: An American snack treat that somehow has morphed into a computer program designed to spy on computer users.

Corruption: One of the fringe benefits of a career in politics.

Cost: The affordable price of something you do not want or the unaffordable price of something that you need.

Cosmopolitan: Pretentious.

Countryside: A place from which impoverished young people are desperate to escape and economically successful middle-aged urban people yearn to settle

Covert: Illegal government activity in the name of security.

Cow: Mass producer of a white liquid intended for calves, consumed mostly by humans.

Crash: Another word hijacked by technology, emerging in a form guaranteed to confuse older generations who do not understand how such a disastrous event could happen to an immobile computer.

Creation: A religious doctrine that teaches us that God created the world and its inhabitants in less than a week, and since proven to be accurate by the fact that only such a hasty piece of work could have produced such a faulty enterprise.

Credit: An evil commercial scheme designed to lure consumers into purchasing goods they do not need and paying for them later at interest rates they cannot afford.

Cricket: A sport invented by Englishmen who had been searching for something to supplement the excitement of drinking tea while eating jam on toast.

Cripple: A word sentenced to solitary confinement by the United States government, followed into seclusion by three successors – "handicapped," "disabled" and "disadvantaged," while the current survivor, "physically challenged," awaits a similar bureaucratic fate.

Crisis: An unpleasant circumstance that eventually will go away to be replaced by another unpleasant circumstance.

Critic: Someone who believes he or she is paid to be a hostile observer of movies, theater and other performing arts.

Critical: A word used by someone to convince others to commit themselves to a policy or venture before it becomes too late, which it rarely does.

Crook: A status that has gained public acceptance among politicians, especially when applied to American presidents, thanks to the nationally televised denial by Richard Nixon that he was one shortly before he was forced to resign from office.

Crowd: A group of people with whom no reasonable person would wish to associate.

Cruelty: Something that humans have refined into an art form.

Cruise: An expensive vacation at sea on a large ship in which people are unable to escape from other people with whom they don't want to associate.

Crusade: An ill-conceived venture eagerly supported by an ill-informed public that becomes educated too late to avert disaster.

C-span: A television network that every person should watch so that they can observe how little time the people they elected to Congress spend doing the work for which they are overpaid.

Cuisine: A fancy name for meals prepared by chefs using mostly sweet sauces in an effort to disguise their inability to cook simply.

Culture: A state of mind in Europe, an inferiority complex in the United States.

Cursor: Once a messenger, now an annoying, but necessary, electronic symbol that seeks to hide in the margins of computer screens to the frustration of people who need it to locate information.

Custard: Another French contribution to the world of inedible cookery.

Customer: Buyers of retail merchandise who have been led to believe that they "are always right" until they read the fine print.

Cute: What women annoyingly use to describe sports cars.

Cynic: A realist.

D

Dagger: Once an effective weapon at close quarters, now used figuratively to describe what is used by ambitious executives in a corporate board room.

Dancing: Something that embarrasses most men, who do it poorly without realizing that many of their female partners and most of the people watching them are unaware of their incompetence.

Danger: A warning of possible harm, curiously used on signs by the management of Heathrow Airport in London to alert washroom visitors to the intensity of the hot water spouting from the taps of the washroom sinks, a problem that would not exist if the temperature was reduced.

Dating: A social occasion involving two persons, at least one of whom will be uncomfortable.

Daze: A condition in which most people exist without realizing it.

Deaf: What some people pretend to be when asked by friends or family members to assist in a physical task.

Death: Blessed nothingness.

Debate: Verbal competition between two or more persons with different views, at least one of whom decides to shout the loudest in a vain effort to win by shielding his or her lack of an argument supported by facts.

Debit: The backbone of a woman's checking account.

Debutante: A wealthy airhead.

Decadence: Invented by the ancient Romans, a form of public entertainment that has been resurrected in the United States.

Decency: A condition that the secretly indecent try to force on others.

Deception: An art eagerly embraced by the willing.

Decision: Something best reached at dawn when no one else is about to offer an opinion.

Declaration: A government pronouncement that signals trouble ahead

Decor: An expensive combination of paint, wallpaper, paintings and furniture that women use to create a desired interior effect, until they tire of it and start all over again.

Decrepit: The condition of someone who has spent too many years in public office.

Defect: Something hidden in a mechanical or electronic device.

Defense: What a government claims it has done, as in "self-defense," after launching a military attack on another country that usually is not able to successfully defend itself.

Defiance: A natural talent of children.

Deficit: The financial system under which governments prefer to operate, to the denunciation of opposition political parties, which continue the practice when they assume power.

Degree: A certificate acknowledging that its bearer is qualified to perform work entitling he or she to earn more money than most people, or to pursue a career flipping burgers or waiting tables at a restaurant.

Delicacy: What food manufacturers label their inedible products.

Delicate: A negotiation in which one side plans to make useless concessions to the other in a deceptive effort to win a major concession that the latter afterward will regret.

Delirium: A condition in which elected officials believe that they have the right to do things until they are caught doing them.

Delivery: Something that is scheduled to occur after a promised date.

Demand: The opening proposal of negotiations, usually offered by the weaker side in an effort to bluff the other into meeting it.

Democracy: A political system in which the voters elect the government they deserve.

Demonstration: The equivalent of trying to draw to an inside straight, as in poker, for an inventor whose creation is about to make its debut.

Demotion: The inevitable fate of a corporate officer.

Denial: The opening shot fired in an excuse leading to a disagreement.

Dentistry: A profession for failed medical students.

Departure: The start of an airline's broken travel promises.

Dependent: Someone who is generally considered a nuisance and often ignored except for a brief period of time when income tax reports become due.

Deployment: Originally a French term used to define the placement of military units, such as France deployed in World Wars I and II, only to have the strategy ignored by the Germans, who invaded from a different direction.

Depose: An effective way of getting rid of a political leader whose policies are hazardous to the health of the public.

Depression: What happens to people who watch the nightly television news.

Desertion: The wishful thought of every soldier facing combat.

Despair: A highly developed skill.

Despot: What people should expect their chief of state to become when he or she is allowed to remain in office too long.

Devastation: The bedroom of a teenage girl.

Developer: Someone who has visions of concrete and glass whenever driving past an open field in the countryside.

Devolution: Evolution in reverse, or what really happened to the apes.

Devotion: Support gone mad.

Detroit: A city that produces second-rate motor vehicles and third-rate football teams.

Devil: An angel in need of counseling.

Diagnosis: A physician's best guess.

Dialogue: A friendly debate, in which intelligence can be guaranteed only when talking to oneself.

Diaper: An undergarment with which people start life as infants and end it as octogenarians.

Diary: A book of memories for people with disorderly minds who, when they've filled all the pages, hide the volume away in an attic or a locked drawer.

Digestion: A biological function that will ultimately rebel when forced to process an excess of fast food.

Dilemma: The price of choice.

Diploma: The poor person's degree.

Disappointment: What optimists get when they take a second look.

Disaster: An opportunity for publishers to sell more newspapers and for television news shows to attract larger than usual audiences.

Discipline: A privilege used by people in authority to punish or force their concept of proper behavior on the physically or economically inferior.

Discotheque: Sometimes referred to as "disco," a once popular meeting place where crowds of the tone deaf could attempt to dance to obnoxious music.

Discreet: Something pledged by someone who should not be told secrets.

Discrimination: What someone will claim after losing a job opportunity to a person of another race or gender, even though the latter may be more competent or experienced.

Disgrace: A condition that government officials and corporate executives have learned to conceal behind cloaks of respectability woven from inflated earnings.

Disguise: Something that should be reserved for children, and only on Halloween.

Disinherited: The fear of every potential heir to a fortune.

Distortion: A political device used by politicians to attack their opponents.

Distraction: Something governments use, such as the suspect excuse of espionage to expel foreign diplomats, in an effort to divert public attention from their own shortcomings.

Distribution: A system in which goods or services are supposed to be made available to the public, but which is guaranteed to fail those people with the greatest need.

District: A geographical area so deliberately convoluted in design, sometimes called "gerrymandering," by politicians in order to insure the election to the United States House of Representatives of a candidate who is a member of their political party.

Disturbance: A knock on the door after dinner.

Divide: Something that is far easier to do than to unite.

Divorce: A very expensive method of ending a marriage in which the only winners are the lawyers who represent the husband and wife.

DNA: A discovery of science that has taken all the fun out of criminal detection.

Documentary: A television motion picture featuring fornicating animals.

Dog: A stupid animal whose servility and dependence have led mistaken humans to bestow on it the title "Man's Best Friend."

Dogma: On the one hand, a curious name for a strong religious belief; on the other, aptly lettered when its syllables are split to provide a two-word phrase.

Dolphin: A mammal that lives in the sea and has the good fortune to be exempt
from the predations of fishermen to the misfortune of other creatures that have just as much right to be there.

Domestic: An illegal alien who is illegally employed to perform household duties at wages and conditions that are sub-standard, usually for a family of means.

Double: Someone paid to pretend to be someone else, thereby freeing the latter from becoming involved in embarrassing or dangerous situations.

Doubt: The highest form of patriotism.

Dove: A gentle winged creature that has been adopted as a symbol by advocates of peace who apparently never have seen a winged hawk in action.

E

Eagerness: The dawn of disappointment.

Early: An embarrassing time for the arrival of guests.

Easter: A Christian celebration of the biblical story of the resurrection of Christ, whose date is a confusing variation from one year to the next because of a formula concocted more than one-thousand years ago by a group of bishops, priests and monks in a meeting at Whitby Abbey, a bleak site in northern England that later helped inspire Bram Stoker to write "Dracula."

Eccentricity: One of the major benefits of old age.

Economist: Someone who makes a living with guesswork.

Ecumenical: A state of truce promoted by religions that will break it at the first opportunity.

Editor: A failed writer.

Education: Society's assault on defenseless children.

Educator: Someone assigned to teach specific subjects to children, without regard to whether he or she ever has had experience in them.

Efficiency: When followed by the word "expert," it forms a phrase describing a person whose recommendations are a roadmap to bankruptcy.

Election: An event in which people believe they are voting for the government they want only to later discover that they got the government they deserved.

Electricity: One of mankind's greatest discoveries put to the worst possible use by guitarists who have no sense of harmony and rhythm.

Elegant: Overdressed.

Elite: People at the top of society, unaware of the dangers below.

Eloquent: Phrases used in speeches by politicians when they have nothing important to say.

E-mail: Electronic miscommunication.

Emasculation: Surgery performed on the male psyche by females.

Embedment: One of the United States Army's most brilliant concepts, it gave news reporters what they believed was a front row seat in combat operations in the early weeks of the invasion of Iraq by assigning them to specific military units. Instead of allowing reporters to acquire inside news tips from officers by covering the combat from the comfort of cafes and bars in Baghdad, as they did in Saigon during the Vietnam War, the plan allowed the Army to control where and when the media representatives would be, thereby limiting the press to narrow, localized views, while avoiding the embarrassment of military failures that could be obtained from a wider view.

Empire: An expansion of a nation's control over lands beyond its borders, always fated to shrink to its humble beginnings as evidenced by the 21st Century edition of the map of the British Empire.

Empower: A buzzword used by movements of groups of people who feel that they are entitled to more regardless of their contributions to society.

Encouragement: What reluctant persons are given by their superiors when urged to perform tasks that the latter never would consider doing themselves.

Encyclopedia: A massive compilation of information presumably covering virtually every subject known to humanity, assembled and written by writers and editors whose research often is based on material that has managed to survive its faulty origins, the result being a publication of suspect data that may become even more suspect when misread or reinterpreted by future researchers.

Endangered: A classification guaranteeing protection to certain species of life with the exemption of humans.

Energy: The oil-based backbone of the United States economy, the dependence on which the government has repeatedly promised since the early nineteen-seventies to reduce by finding less costly alternatives, while allowing the public and industry to consume petroleum in increasingly greater volume.

English: Obviously the easiest language to learn, simply because so many people whose native languages are something else are able to learn how to speak it, while people whose native language it is rarely are able to speak anything else, as is the case with British and Americans.

Enterprising: What someone in the business world is credited with being when he orshe makes a lot of money from an idea stolen from someone else.

Enthusiasm: The adolescence of cynicism.

Environment: A highly charged political cause among voters, but a bore to elected officials and the news media.

Ephemeral: Public confidence in its government.

Epic: A word used by book publishers and movie producers to stir interest in novels and motion pictures that are so lengthy that they are guaranteed to bore readers and film audiences.

Epitaph: An untruth etched into the tombstone of someone who would be embarrassed to read it if he or she were alive.

Equality: Something preached by the powerful to the well-founded disbelief of the disenfranchised.

Escape: Something that tempts everyone at least once in a lifetime.

Escargot: Proof that the French will eat anything that flies, swims, walks, runs, crawls or slithers.

Espionage: A profession in which spies are employed by governments to spy on other spies, who would be jobless if they had applied for work in another field.

Eternity: A place of condemnation for any living thing.

Ethics: Extinct components of professional codes of behavior.

Etiquette: Artificial manners.

Euthanasia: A humane way to end the suffering of animals, yet forbidden as a treatment for the suffering of humans.

Evasive: A deft maneuver at which most politicians are skilled.

Evil: Good's fun-loving brother.

Evolution: The thinking man's version of the Old Testament.

Exact: A word increasingly and wrongly used on broadcast shows and commercials before the phrase "the same thing," because it means "the same thing."

Examination: The moment of truth for students nearing graduation and would-be professionals seeking licensing.

Excrement: Politics.

Excuse: Something that becomes less convincing in quantity.

Execution: Legalized homicide.

Exemption: A status that legislators afford themselves when adopting laws designed to apply to everyone else.

Exercise: Something diligently avoided by thinking people.

Exhibition: A showing in a fixed setting where an artist can display his or her lack of talent to a gullible public.

Exotic: Anything new that has no practical value.

Expatriate: Someone dissatisfied enough to leave a native country and settle in another where he or she can complain endlessly about the society they abandoned to people who really do not care.

Expectation: Disappointment waiting to happen.

Experiment: A deliberate attempt at failure.

Expert: A title given to a repeat guest on a television talk show.

Exploitation: The natural course of events controlled by government and industry.

Export: When coupled with the word "import," a company where business often is dedicated to exporting money and importing illegal substances.

Extemporaneous: An impromptu form of speech that is almost guaranteed to make a politician look foolish.

Extra: An incentive that a buyer does not need, but which is added to a prospective purchase by a salesman eager to close a deal.

F

Fabulous: A word used mostly in Hollywood to describe almost everything.

Facts: Details ignored by journalists, law enforcement officers and attorneys.

Factory: Where people do an honest day's work for a dishonest day's pay.

Fallible: Formal pronouncements or religious doctrine.

Fame: Something followed first by fortune, then by obscurity.

Familiarity: Something that can be enjoyed only when taken sparingly.

Family: Considered for centuries to be the fabric of social society, in reality it usually is a dysfunctional group of eccentrics.

Famine: The condition of a large percentage of the population of a poor country, whose situation is publicly decried by more prosperous nations that are willing to help only to the degree that their own political and economic interests are not disrupted.

Fantasy: A world in which all people take an occasional vacation.

Father: Someone whose status has been downgraded from the parent who "knows best" to the person who hasn't got a clue.

Fatigue: The logical result of an average day.

Favor: A debt that usually is asked to be repaid at the most awkward moment.

Fence: A place with seats reserved for politicians who lack convictions.

Festival: Retail business disguised as entertainment.

Fetish: A practice that people will publicly decry as unnatural even while secretly practicing the same thing or something similar.

Fidelity: Something that someone who has been intimately unfaithful in a relationship expects of their partner or spouse.

File: A place where records and other information are left to die.

Filibuster: A political tactic in which members of the minority party will speak for days in an effort to thwart the majority from passing legislation, but rarely used simply because it would require elected members of the United States Senate to actually spend more time on the floor of their Capitol chamber rather than in their favorite tavern.

Finger: Once simply one of the 10 extremities of the human hand, now part of modern folklore when the middle one of either hand is extended in what is called "giving the finger" to someone as an expression of irritation.

Finland: A country where people without a sense of humor can feel comfortable.

Fit: A state claimed that people can achieve with exercise when, in reality, it is a condition likely to suddenly strike those who physically exert themselves.

Flag: Originally a banner around which soldiers who were losing a battle could rally, now a symbol of national pride that sometimes is misused by politicians to further controversial causes.

Flash: The excessive use of ostentation to cover social flaws.

Flattery: Tactics used by incompetents seeking employment, job promotion or salary increases.

Flaw: Something that exists in every argument made by the other person.

Flimsy: A product described as "solid" by a salesperson.

Flip-flops: Florida's contribution to the world of fashion.

Flogging: Punishment no longer permitted in all but a handful of societies, where the crime rate is below average.

Flood: An event that should be expected by people who complain of drought.

Florida: Home of the newlywed and the nearly dead.

Flowers: Something women should be wary of when given to them by men.

Fluff: The substance of a political speech.

Focus: A discipline that has been all but lost to a public whose attention span has become limited.

Folly: The end-of-the-year spending orgy of the United States Congress, during which taxpayers are expected to pick up the tab for such silliness as studies of the migration habits of earthworms and the construction of roads that lead to wilderness dead-ends.

Football: A highly profitable non-academic venture undertaken by academic institutions.

Force: Something that governments will threaten to use against weaker nations in order to prevent them from agreeing to compromises.

Foreclosure: What people can expect will happen to the property they purchased but could not afford, despite meeting the criteria that a lender had assured would qualify them for a loan that they would not be able to repay.

Forefathers: Ancestor settlers who amassed considerable fortunes by obtaining large tracts of property without payment thanks to grants from a king or queen, or by swindling natives.

Forest: A wooded area where deer, rabbits and other dangerous creatures are hunted by men armed with rifles.

Forgive: A word used to subtly imply control over a person who has repented his or her role in a perceived wrong, when the more magnanimous response would be to simply reassure faith in the latter.

Forward: A direction in which politicians are always proclaiming that others should go while they stand still.

Fraction: The part of a number still taught in schools in a handful of countries, including the United States, which steadfastly refuses to convert to the simple metrics system where confusing fractions do not exist.

Fragile: A word that, when labeled on the outside of a package being shipped by the United States Postal Service, increases the chances that the contents will be damaged.

France: A home for expatriates from other countries who are willing to bear the pretensions of the locals determined to hang onto faded glories.

Franchise: An independently owned business selling retail goods or services at an outlet with a nationally recognized name, thereby diluting the quality and service that people no longer expect, but once received, from local establishments that had no prepackaged corporate oversight.

Frankfurter: Also known as a "hot dog," an American sausage made from cow, pig, chicken or turkey parts that no one would consider buying separately.

Free: Something that usually has no value.

Freedom: A word found in the lyrics of patriotic music sung by the military.

Freelance: A career path for people whose overabundance of imagination is equaled only by their overdrawn bank accounts.

Fresco: A type of art praised simply because it has been painted directly onto a wall by an artist who took payment from his or her patrons while knowing that climatological factors eventually destroy frescoes.

Friend: Someone who brings you bad news created by your enemy.

Frivolous: The condition of a teenage girl.

Frugal: A kindly description of a skinflint.

Fugitive: Someone on the run from the justice system, sometimes innocent, always with good reason.

Fumble: The nightmare of an American football player whose task is to run with the ball.

Funeral: A costly and elaborate celebration of death at which someone who has passed away is extolled for virtues he or she lacked during life, and attended by family, friends and others, most of whom would not bother to be at the affair had the deceased not been wealthy.

Futility: An attempt at getting information by telephone from a government agency.

Future: A time where the worst waits to make an appearance.

G

Gadget: The latest in useless electronics.

Gain: Ill-gotten when obtained by someone of wealth or power.

Galaxy: One of billions of large masses in outer space, each containing billions of stars, offering hope that intelligent life might exist somewhere in the universe.

Gallantry: Self-serving politeness.

Gallows: A device that has achieved romantic status among people who believe in the execution of people accused of crimes, whether guilty or innocent.

Gang: Urban marauders.

Garden: A place where plants that you wish would grow do not, while providing a haven for plants that you wish did not.

Gay: A word that somehow took on a new meaning in the middle of the 20th Century.

Geek: Someone so enamored of technology that he or she spends so much money on every new gadget that they are forced to live with their parents or in lodgings that have little furniture, and near-empty food cabinets and refrigerators.

Geezer: A once perfectly acceptable word for geriatrics.

General: A title granted to military officers destined to prove their lack of imagination in the use of strategy and tactics.

Generation: If younger, frowned upon by the elderly; if older, ignored by the young.

Generosity: An act that never should be expected.

Genius: An unofficial title given to people whose many failures are forgotten when they finally develop the one idea that is accepted by others, even though its worth may remain unproven.

Gentleman: Someone who dines rather than eats.

Gentrification: A government term for a form of urban renewal in which needy people are evicted from homes that are scheduled to be converted into upscale living quarters for people who can afford to reside in them.

Germany: A country in which visitors should never use the word "war."

Gesture: The lost art of being magnanimous, replaced by a variety of physical movements intended solely for insults.

Ghetto: An area where the government consigns the poor to reside.

Gibberish: The language of the legal profession.

Gift: Something that a purchaser likes, believing that the person for whom he or she is obtaining it will equally enjoy it.

Gigolo: Nice work for men who can get it.

Girl: A female who cannot wait to be a woman, at which point she realizes that the benefits of maturity are outweighed by those that she left behind.

Giver: Someone who is ripe for exploitation by a taker.

Glamour: An artificial attempt at beauty sought by attractive women.

Glitter: The facade of Las Vegas.

Gloom: Heaven for cynics.

Glory: Sought mostly by men, a status that is usually achieved at great cost to those who do not seek it.

Gluttony: A deadly virtue.

God: A supreme being that man has created in his own image.

Gold: A metal with little practical use that is valued because 5,000 years ago it was praised and prized by a forgotten Egyptian pharaoh.

Golf: Walking in the guise of a sport.

Gospel: Ancient fiction.

Gossip: The favorite pastime of men and women who seem to know everything about everyone but themselves.

Gourmet: A person who has taken an enjoyable path to obesity.

Government: A privileged monarchy with electronic communications.

Grammar: Something no longer taught in public schools.

Grandchildren: Gifts to older persons who have waited years to get even with their children.

Grapes: Fruit fit for consumption only when they have been mashed into fermented liquid.

Grass: A good reason for living in an apartment building.

Gratitude: Something to express in return for what other people believe is a favor they have given, especially when its expression helps to insure more favors in the future.

Gravy: A sauce so hazardous to health that it surely must have earned its name from that good, old-fashioned word "graveyard."

Gray: The favorite color of liberals.

Great: A word whose value has been diminished by its inflationary application to persons whose success usually is limited to avoiding failure.

Grocery: A victim of suburban supermarkets.

Group: Three or more persons who bond together because they believe they share common interests only to discover, usually too late, they have little in common, after all.

Grudge: Something that women cling to with tenacity.

Guess: An ability without which analysts would be unemployed.

Guide: A person who will lead people to where they do not want to go.

Guilt: The assumption, contrary to legal propaganda, that someone on trial for a crime is presumed to be, thereby making it necessary for the accused to prove his or her innocence.

Gum: An inedible substance whose use is made annoying to others by people who insist on chewing it with their mouths open.

Guzzle: A method of drinking liquid, mastered mostly by men who drink beer from a can or bottle.

H

Haggis: Considered a delicacy in Scotland, a prepared dish that looks as objectionable as it tastes.

Hallucination: Reality to someone who has smoked too much marijuana.

Handbag: A portable fabric or leather container carried by women into which they have stuffed as many items as possible that they never will need on their daily rounds.

Handicap: Something women who seek equality with men claim when participating in a mixed gender sports event.

Handwriting: An illegible method of written communication practiced mostly by people who haven't learned to spell.

Haphazard: Something unpredictable, such as the initial implementation of a government program.

Harbinger: A word designed to precede the word "doom."

Harassment: What viewers of television are subjected to during commercial breaks.

Harem: A playground for leaders of Turkey and the Arab world in days gone by.

Harmless: Something sought by lawmakers intent on declaring it illegal.

Haste: Business in the 21st Century.

Hate: The purest of emotions.

Headcheese: A meat sold at delicatessen counters; a vile sandwich ingredient, containing nothing resembling cheese but, instead scrap pieces of the heads of slaughtered animals held together by inedible gelatin.

Headline: That part of a newspaper that promises more than can be delivered by the news article that it heralds.

Health: Something people ignore until they begin to experience pain.

Hearing: A public event at which politicians collect information that is committed to paper used to fill empty shelves.

Hearsay: The first edition of television news.

Heir: Someone waiting for a wealthy relative to die.

Hell: A place designed by an architect who specializes in building airports.

Helmet: Headgear originally intended to protect a person's head, but now used as a weapon in American football.

Heresy: The thinking person's religion.

Hermit: Someone who has refined the practice of peace and quiet into an art.

Hero: An ordinary person, who once achieved fame through an act of bravery undertaken in a moment of temporary insanity, but who can earn the title in the 21st Century simply by doing nothing more heroic than being in a place he or she does not wish to be.

Hibernation: A sensible practice of certain wild animals that humans could do well to emulate.

Highways: Wide roads designed to allow motorists to drive long distances at high speeds, while allowing an acceptable rate of accidents resulting in serious injury and death.

History: Past events as recalled by the winners of conflicts.

Hitler: History's proof that public support is easy to manipulate.

Hoarding: What consumers do at supermarkets when a faced with the possibility of an impending natural disaster.

Hobby: A waste of time for workaholics, sanity insurance for thinking people.

Hobo: Called "king of the road," someone who is secretly envied by men.

Hollywood: Heaven for wedding planners and divorce lawyers.

Holy: A promotional label attached to religious rituals and artifacts.

Home: A place where a man can drink to his liver's content.

Homeland: A word government uses in place of the name of its country in the belief it will inspire public support for controversial measures.

Homeless: A person who knows how to beat the system of landlords and mortgages.

Hometown: A place where your friends are chosen for you rather than being chosen by you.

Homework: A device employed by incompetent teachers.

Honesty: A policy rarely considered by politicians to be the best.

Honorable: A title mistakenly used when formally addressing a politician who has been elected to legislative office.

Hope: A tragedy waiting to happen.

Horoscope: Babble concocted for the gullible.

Horse: For centuries it has allowed men and women to push it to extremes of speed and distance while riding on its back, thereby earning it first place in the race for the world's dumbest being, followed by the sheep and turkey, with humans having moved up to fourth place in a valiant effort to overtake the trio.

Hospital: An institution that must meet a set quota of the number of ill patients that it kills every year.

Hotel: A much-needed refuge from home.

Housekeeping: A task that men ignore and women attend to when threatened with the imminent arrival of guests.

Human: A complex living machine that works poorly because of one flawed part – its brain.

Humane: A polite word that society attaches to the execution of convicted criminals.

Humility: A condition feared by persons concerned about their public image.

Humor: Laughter at the expense of someone or something.

Hunter: Someone who kills wild animals for the heck of it.

Hydrant: A device that allows people in major cities to gain the relief from extreme summer heat that inadequate rental apartment air conditioning has failed to provide.

Hygiene: A practice that has become so pervasive in the United States that it has led to the removal of the natural flavor from food.

Hyphen: A respectable punctuation mark that semi-literates of the computer age generation are rapidly consigning to oblivion.

Hypocrisy: The art of being pleasant in social situations.

Hysterics: A woman's undeniable right.

I

Ice: Frozen water which, in the form of cubes, will tamper with the taste of good whiskey.

Iconoclast: Someone who wants to change the world for the better.

Idea: A threat to the established order.

Idealism: A philosophy for fools.

Identical: An imprecise adjective since nothing on Earth is truly identical.

Identity: Something that requires such careful guarding in the 21st Century because computer crime has led to the creation of an electronic industry that preys upon people with promises of identity theft protection, which it cannot guarantee.

Idiot: A person who praises everything.

Idleness: A fringe benefit that labor unions obtain for their members.

Idolatry: Limited to pagan religious practice in ancient times, it has become a ritual of the public worship of entertainers and athletes.

Ignorance: A subject taught in public schools.

Illegible: The handwriting of physicians.

Illicit: Something that encourages people to do things that they otherwise never would consider.

Illiterate: Most of the population.

Illusion: Good government.

Illustrious: An unofficial title used to add prestige to pompous politicians campaigning for election to public office.

Imagination: A hostage of television shows and video games.

Imitate: What people do when they feel inadequate.

Immediately: A request or demand for the expeditious completion of a task that will be delayed.

Immigrant: Someone willing to do the dirty work that citizens of his or her host country will not, regardless of the economic consequences and the demagoguery of populist politicians.

Immortality: The dream of everyone which, if achieved, would become a nightmare of boredom.

Immovable: The position of the other person during a dispute.

Impeachment: A process which, if used more frequently, might have the effect of keeping politicians from abusing the privilege of public office.

Impersonation: Live comedy on the political campaign trail.

Important: Something tangible or intangible whose value is determined by the belief of the person who knows about or owns it.

Imported: A marketing word used by retailers to convince consumers to spend more money for products bearing labels that they hail from a foreign country and, therefore, are of higher quality, which is often the case. The excessive prices charged for such products are not the result of shipping costs or import duties, as claimed by businesses, but simply the result of greed taking advantage of public ignorance.

Impress: What people attempt to do in order to cover their shortcomings,

Improved: A marketing word designed to sell what usually is a new and inferior version of an already established popular product.

Improbable: Something that cannot be explained by someone who lacks imagination.

Impulsiveness: An annoying quality that somehow works for people who ask questions after doing something equally annoying.

Inch: The length of the thumb above the first joint of a 16th Century English king that set the standard for a ridiculous system of measurement that has been all but abandoned in England and ignored by the rest of the world except the United States.

Incompetence: A skill awaiting self-discovery.

Incompatibility: The natural order of things.

Indebted: What politicians become when taking campaign contributions from powerful special interests.

Indecision: A state into which most people retreat when faced with options.

Indelicacy: The art of plain speaking.

Independent: Someone who refuses to be a member of a political party because he or she is aware of the dangers of such affiliation.

India: A country where poverty can equal success.

Indifference: What can be expected from politicians the day after they have been elected to public office.

Indignation: A mild form of outrage, usually expressed by people who believe that their genealogy prohibits them from making stronger displays of emotion.

Individualist: A person who understands the perils of group discussion.

Infantry: Soldiers who foot the bill for the mistakes of generals.

Inferior: Anything that is too complex for anyone to understand.

Information: Something most people seem to feel that they can do without.

Ingrate: What a politician becomes after being elected.

Ingratiate: What an ambitious subordinate will seek to do with his or her superior.

Inhumane: Human treatment of animals used for food.

Injured: Once a misfortune that occurred to civilians, the word was adopted by the United States military when it invaded Iraq in 2003 as a substitute for the word "wounded," which the public opinion spinners at the Pentagon felt was too closely associated with the realities of combat.

Injustice: A day in court.

Innocence: A claim made by most guilty people brought before a courtroom judge.

Insensitivity: The first refuge of a journalist.

Insignificant: Television dialogue.

Insinuate: A form of accusation that can be denied when its user feels it is opportune.

Insistent: The prelude to a tantrum.

Insolence: Disagreement in class-conscious societies,

Insulation: Something with which White House aides try to surround the President of the United States in an effort to shield their boss from criticism, the result of which is to desensitize the Chief Executive to the reality of public opinion.

Insurance: Legalized gambling.

Institution: A status that can be achieved by something that lasts beyond its useful time.

Instructions: A complex document of poorly worded details often accompanied by misleading illustrations that come with a purchased household device fiendishly manufactured so that it requires frustrating hours of assembly by its buyer.

Insufferable: What someone experiences when cornered at a party by a person who talks incessantly about his or her career.

Integrity: Something political candidates promise to restore if they are elected to public office, only to be forgotten once they get there.

Intelligence: Something humans have sought so relentlessly that they have had to extend their search deep into outer space in the hope that it might exist somewhere in the universe.

Intentions: The first step on the path to disaster.

Interest: An amount of money that a bank is stingy in dispensing to borrowers, while generous to itself in receipt of what it charges for lending services.

Interference: Good intentions of someone seeking to advise friends and relatives.

Intermission: The most eagerly awaited part of a boring theatrical production, allowing spectators to drink themselves into a condition that allows them to mentally survive the rest of the show.

Intern: Someone whose abilities are exploited for no financial remuneration.

Internet: Technology created to educate the public via an "information super-highway" that government and private industry have converted into an electronic toll road.

Interview: A high form of intimidation.

Interruption: What people hope for when cornered at a party by an obnoxious guest.

Intrigue: The currency of government, particularly in the field of foreign affairs.

Intuition: A woman's version of guesswork

Invincible: A belief that belligerent nations have in their armed forces, forgetting that Soviet Union dictator Josef Stalin once said of the approaching Germans during World War II – "history proves that there are no invincible armies."

Invitation: Something denied to people who want it most.

Ireland: A place whose citizens stubbornly refuse to admit that they are part of Britain, whose government is equally stubborn in its refusal to admit that it no longer rules Ireland.

Irony: Something that is deficient in most people, especially those who make an annoying habit of seeking public recognition.

Irresponsible: What can be expected of teenagers.

IRS: The three most feared letters of the alphabet in the United States.

Island: Considered an idyllic place to live by those who reside elsewhere.

Italy: The ideal country, where the government is reluctant to collect taxes in fear that any such attempt will encourage the people to throw it out of office.

J

Janitor: The most valuable employee of government and industry.

Jargon: The official language of government.

Jaywalk: Something people will do regardless of the danger from motor vehicle traffic even when the safety of a crosswalk is less than a few seconds away.

Jeans: Once the inexpensive clothing of the poor, now the expensive clothing of the affluent, thanks to creative marketing.

Jesus: One of history's greatest figures, he is worshiped by followers of a religion that he neither practiced nor preached, yet was founded in his name, and ignored by followers of the religion that he had both practiced and preached.

Jewelry: Ornaments made with metal, and bright or colored stones with little practical value, but are highly treasured by persons who believe that wearing these trinkets improves their physical appearance or gives them an air of importance.

Jogging: An exercise that guarantees the future employment of osteopathic surgeons and morticians.

Joke: A humorous short story or deed based on insulting someone or something.

Journalist: A creative writer.

Judas: The most misunderstood of the Twelve Apostles.

Judge: A person appointed or elected to make decisions based on law, but who usually makes them based on personal or political considerations.

Jump: A word some people will shout when someone else is threatening to leap from a height that will cause the latter severe physical injury or death.

Jungle: Once a vast tract of land covered with dense foliage that hid dangerous beasts, but now little more than a cuddly rainforest.

Junk: What buyers can expect to find at yard sales.

Junket: A journey undertaken by members of the United States Congress, purportedly for fact-finding purposes, but in reality an expensive vacation financed by gullible taxpayers.

Jurisdiction: A right claimed by one group of people over a geographic area populated by others seeking to resist the former, except when the issue involves law enforcement when both sides will seek to pass the buck to the other.

Jury: Citizens who would prefer to be elsewhere.

Justice: Legal revenge.

K

Kansas: A place to go when the end of the world is near because everything happens there ten years later.

Karaoke: A musical system that allows people who have had too much to drink in bars and pubs to make fools of themselves by attempting to sing.

Ketchup: A thick liquid used mostly by Americans to ruin food such as steak and eggs.

Kidding: A word used by people in an attempt to extricate themselves from embarrassing situations after having insulted someone who can make their lives uncomfortable.

Killing: Something that humans admire in predatory animals such as hawks and tigers as long as these creatures confine their activity to their normal prey.

Kilt: A short skirt woven in a tartan pattern that Scotsmen enjoy wearing in the coldest weather.

King: The only actor who is allowed to sit in a Shakespearean play.

Kipper: An inedible fish that is served almost exclusively at breakfast in Scotland, thereby all but destroying the desire of anyone who is not Scottish to eat for the rest of the day.

Knickerbockers: A perfectly good nickname given to the New York professional basketball team when it was founded in the nineteen-forties, but since officially shortened to the meaningless "Knicks."

Knife: Something a superstar professional athlete attempts to hold to the throat of a team owner at contract renewal time.

Knighthood: An honor once reserved for men who supposedly had performed memorable deeds of valor and chivalry, but now awarded to bureaucrats and musicians.

Knowledge: Something that someone with limited intelligence can be credited with having simply by quoting the sayings of people who actually possess it.

L

Lackey: Someone with political connections who is employed as an aide to a high ranking elected official.

Lady: A title that has been a casualty of the women's rights movement.

Landlord: The worst management job in the housing industry.

Landscape: A type of painting done by an artist with little talent and no imagination..

Language: A means of miscommunication.

Late: A preferred alternative to early.

Latin: An ancient language mistakenly believed to help people better understand English, but used almost exclusively by doctors and lawyers to confuse the public.

Laughter: Something that should be prohibited to people who do not also sometimes laugh at their own absurdities.

Laws: Rules dictating behavior for the general public, while providing exemptions for those legislators who adopted them.

Lawyer: Someone whose study of the law is endowed with the remarkable ability to help clients avoid the consequences breaking it.

Leash: A metal chain or leather rope originally designed for keeping dogs tethered, but now more often used by wives to keep husbands in tow.

Leave: What parents wish their children would do when they reach the legal age of maturity.

Lecture: Something that thinking people avoid.

Lechery: A hobby for old men.

Legend: A status that professional athletes seek to achieve in their own time.

Lesson: Something that teachers attempt to impress upon their students without realizing that lessons cannot be taught, but must be learned.

Letter: Future trouble when written to a lover or lawyer.

Liar: Everyone, at one time or another.

Libel: Character assassination that judicial rulings have allowed to newspapers.

Liberal: Someone who refuses to recognize blame and is supportive of poverty, mostly because he or she lacks the financial resources of a conservative.

Libertarian: An anarchist with restraint.

Library: A good alternative to public schools.

License: A piece of paper which, when purchased from a government, allows the bearer to perform specific tasks that otherwise would be criminal acts.

Life: A comedy of errors.

Lighter: A device, powered by chemicals, designed to ruin whatever enjoyment of taste is found by smokers of cigarettes, cigars or pipe tobacco.

Limbo: The third planet from the sun.

Limited: A word that has been a victim of inflation, especially when used as a marketing term to convince gullible consumers to purchase "limited numbered editions" of art prints and ceramics that are produced in quantities of thousands, thus diluting whatever resale value they are advertised as having.

Limp: The foundation of an excuse.

Lingerie: Sinning clothes.

Literacy: A goal that cannot be achieved in the public schools.

Literature: A style of writing found in books that do not become best-sellers.

Litigation: America's national pastime in which judges are the umpires, lawyers are the managers, and plaintiffs and defendants always are stranded on base at the end of the game.

Logistics: A vital military function in which supplies needed by soldiers doing the fighting are sent to areas where there is no combat.

Logjam: Something to expect from a session of legislators elected to pass laws.

Loser: The person or team that makes the biggest contribution to the winner.

Lottery: A game of chance in which millions of people spend money that could be used to improve the economy but, instead, enriches only a tiny fraction of the public and most of the government bureaucracy.

Love: A disease so pervasive that medical science long ago realized it would be a waste of money and research trying to find a cure for it.

Lover: A person so close that he or she is just waiting to pounce on you should you cross that thin line separating love from hate.

Loyalty: The first victim of ambition.

Luck: The whipping boy of failure.

Luggage: Unless carried on an airplane by passengers, something that an airline does not guarantee that it will be delivered to its intended destination.

Luxury: An expensive illusion of social status and comfort.

M

Machine: A mechanical device certain to stop functioning when most needed.

Magazine: A publication which allows its writers to take greater license with the truth than newspapers allow its reporters.

Magnanimity: Something no longer extended by the victors to the losers.

Mail: Written messages paid for without guarantee of delivery.

Maintenance: Service that never is available when required.

Mall: Bad taste in retail shopping design.

Malpractice: Something that is performed on clients every day by physicians and lawyers.

Mandate: A right claimed by all elected politicians, even when they have reached office with less than fifty percent of voter support.

Mania: An expression of public sentiment at athletic events.

Manifesto: A document that should be distrusted by the public.

Mansion: A large house where two people can live without the inconvenience of having to see each other.

Manure: Animal biological waste that is used to feed fruits and vegetables that later are sold by grocery stores to the public as "organic."

Map: Ancient Egyptian hieroglyphics to women.

Marriage: A state of indifference.

Margarine: A vegetable-based imitation of butter, whose sale to the public is falsely promoted by its producers as just as flavorful as the latter, proving that people get what they pay for.

Mart: A suffix added to one or more letters to create the name of a large and annoying retail store that sells inferior merchandise to consumers who believe they are getting bargains.

Martyr: Someone who becomes a poster boy for a cause after needlessly giving his or her life for what usually turns out to be nothing.

Mash: A method used by some cooks to ruin potatoes.

Mask: Something worn on the face of politicians when they are scheduled to appear in public.

Matches: Tools of an arsonist.

Materialism: The mass religion of the 21st Century.

Mathematics: Arithmetic without the basics.

Maturity: A painful duty for anyone past the age of 29 years.

Mayday: Associated with air travel, a shouted signal warning of imminent disaster, during which passengers are expected to remember the safety precautions they were supposed to learn at takeoff, while plunging 30,000 feet from the sky into land or sea.

Meaningful: Something that can be found as easily as a needle in a haystack.

Mechanic: Once a respectable job title that helped people needing the help of one know exactly what they were getting, since replaced by "engineer," "specialist" and "expert."

Medal: An award concocted centuries ago to reward soldiers for bravery in combat in order to inspire their comrades with incentives to seek similar awards by performing military actions that they otherwise would have no intention of doing.

Medicine: A branch of science dedicated to sending out into the world professionals who lack the verbal skills necessary to communicate life and death information to the average person.

Mediocrity: The 21st Century standard for excellence.

Meek: People who are going to be disappointed when they finally realize that they are not going to inherit the Earth.

Meeting: A waste of government and corporate productivity.

Melodrama: An emotional perfromance at which women excel.

Memory: Something with which the elderly are blessed by recalling what they believe are the happier times of their youth or are cursed with when they realize that such times never occurred.

Mercenary: An unreliable soldier of unknown capability.

Merger: A polite term for the joining of two companies, in which the weaker sees its assets absorbed, its employees' jobs eliminated and its name disappear.

Metrics: A system of measurement ignored by Americans who, unless they learn it, could someday find themselves near the bottom of the world's economy.

Mexico: An employment agency for the United States.

Midwest: The central area of the United States, which was settled by pioneers who lacked the will or stamina to go further west.

Might: A polite word for "force."

Military: An organization recruited by a government and used primarily to destroy other governments either for aggression or self-defense.

Millions: Once all but impossible for the average person to visualize when used to describe a quantity of money, it has been made so insignificant by reckless government spending that the next level of billions is certain to follow it on the path to mathematical obscurity.

Mime: An annoying form of entertainment.

Mincemeat: A a concoction of sweet and ingredients that contains no meat.

Minority: A group of citizens who can have greater influence than the majority in a democracy, usually because they are right.

Minute: A unit of time in which people commit themselves to doing something that takes longer.

Miracle: A word science attaches to a new drug before its use is found to have hazardous consequences on people for whom it is prescribed.

Mirror: A device in which people can see their reflection altered horizontally from their left from to their right, while begging the question: shouldn't their reflection also be altered vertically so that their head is at the bottom?

Miscalculation: The inevitable surprise that befalls armed aggression.

Mischief: Something that every child should experience at least once.

Mission: Something that someone who is asked to undertake should think at least twice before declining to do so.

Mistake: Something that people produce beyond their daily quota.

Model: A semi-emaciated female who, for some reason, is believed by the fashion industry to be the only type of person able to demonstrate outrageous clothing for sale to women who lack the physical appearance or the audacity to wear it.

Moderation: A style of life that never should be practiced for more than a day or two a year.

Modesty: Something behind which people with superiority complexes hide.

Moment: An infinitesimal slice of time, during which opportunity often becomes available but is missed.

Monastery: A place where the clergy should be kept from view of the public.

Money: Originally a simple medium of exchange, it has evolved into a much-sought commodity.

Monogamy: One spouse too many.

Monopoly: The dream of every business.

Morality: A tool with which those who lack the imagination to be wicked use to condemn those who do not.

Morass: A place where elected legislators hide from public view while they pretend to make an effort to work out their differences over the wording of proposed new laws.

Morons: Beings whose name was mispronounced "Martians" when they were expected to invade Earth in the mid-20th Century, but already had been here and, with their descendants, have been running the world ever since.

Morsel: A small piece of usually flavorful food that leaves people who sample it wanting more than is available.

Mortician: Someone who preys on the sentiments of people who have lost a loved one through death by using his or her creative ability to give the corpse a pleasant appearance and a send-off worthy of Hollywood, all at great expense to the bereaved.

Mother: A woman who doesn't know how to cook a palatable meal.

Motorcycle: A two-wheeled vehicle, one of whose riders is death.

Mouse: An annoying computer navigation device without hair.

Movie: Expensive entertainment designed to reflect real life, but produced and performed by people with little knowledge of reality.

Mulch: A product mostly used by American gardeners who are too lazy to pull weeds.

Municipality: A small unit of government where politicians can hone the skills they will need to deceive the public on their way to higher office.

Mystery: A word that people attach to something they do not take the time to understand, especially in connection with religion.

Mystic: Someone who believes that contemplation and doing nothing will lead to world peace.

Mythology: The final resting place of defunct religions.

N

Naive: Someone who believes government works for the welfare of the people.

Napoleon: The last capable French military leader.

Nation: People who are bonded by a common political system despite the inconvenience of incompetent and disinterested leaders.

Natural: Everything that exists or occurs on Earth, despite efforts of the majority, which insists on classifying as unnatural, behavior with which it does not agree.

Nature: Meteorological violence that strikes after lulling its victims into a sense of false security by providing them with landscapes of beauty.

Nausea: What someone experiences while watching a political debate.

Navigator: Once an indispensable specialist who had the responsibility of providing the best possible route for long-haul ships and airplanes, made all but extinct in the 21st Century by a computerized machine that can do the same job as long as the electrical, battery or software systems do not fail.

Necktie: A cloth ornament that men are required to wear tied around their necks for certain occasions at the expense of comfort.

Neglect: What men and women can expect from each other after they are married.

Negotiation: Extreme fighting with words.

Neighbor: Someone who can be tolerated as long as he or she remains on the other side of the fence.

Nepotism: A right which relatives of elected officials believe they have earned, and often are granted, simply because of their family ties.

Nero: Emperor of Rome reputed to have fiddled while the city burned, a slur leveled by incompetent historians who have failed to recognize his genius as the founder of urban renewal.

Neurosis: An infectious disease that becomes a public epidemic during the final days of a political election campaign.

News: Information, sometimes in the guise of fiction, often in need of correction, always awaiting revision.

Newscaster: Someone on television who reads news gathered and written by others, and whose only qualification for the job is physical appeal to viewers.

Newspaper: An inconvenient means of keeping up with the news, not only because it is a publication of awkward size, but also because it requires that readers must wash their hands to rid themselves of ink residue after reading it.

Newspeak: Concocted by George Orwell to describe the ambiguous language of the repressive government of his novel "1984," it has since been adopted by all 21st Century governments, as evidenced by the pronouncements of its leaders.

Nickname: A form of identification which people use to mask a name that they consider to be embarrassing.

Night: That part of a day without the dubious benefits of sunshine.

Nightmares: Adventuresome dreams worth the price of sleep.

No: A word so rarely used by parents that their children do not understand its meaning by the time they have grown into their teen years.

Noble: Moronic.

Nomination: Once an intriguing process that political bosses settled in smoke-filled rooms to choose the best political party candidates for high public office. Over the years, it has evolved into a series of primaries in which voters choose the most charismatic and, usually, least qualified candidates while, at the same time insuring the staging of boring political conventions ignored by the majority of the population.

Nonsense: Someone else's ideas.

Noon: The hour at which the Washington press corps begins its journey into inebriation.

Normal: What the majority likes to call itself.

Nostalgia: A romantic vision of how bad things once were.

Nothing: The sum of the memorable lifetime achievements of most people.

Nourishment: Something lacking in the diet of fast-food America.

Novel: Book-length fiction that denies any resemblance of real persons to its characters, while basing its most ludicrous of the latter on people that the author knows.

Nuclear: Governments usually follow this word with the word "energy" when what they really are thinking is the word "weapons."

Nudist: A person who would not dare to bare his or her body unclothed in the company of friends and relatives, but will do so in a private camp where fellow nudists feel perfectly comfortable exposing their physical defects to each other.

Nuisance: Anything that interrupts someone's train of trivial thought.

Numerology: Another of the many bogus sciences that somehow has managed to attract legions of gullible followers.

Nun: A woman willing to publicize her fear of femininity which, should what she refers to as her calling lead her to the parochial school teaching path, is likely to result in her physically taking her frustrations out on her students.

O

Oath: A solemn pledge sometimes carrying the force of law, which often is taken by someone with no intention of keeping it.

Oats: A grain that is widely used to feed horses, but also is sold as an inedible high-priced breakfast ingredient to be consumed with undrinkable cow's milk by people.

Obesity: A widely condemned health hazard for the general public, yet a highly praised virtue for Japanese sumo wrestlers and American football offensive linemen.

Obey: What husbands must do when their wives speak.

Obituary: A newspaper article summarizing the dubious accomplishments of a dead person while ignoring their failures.

Objection: The cry of a defense lawyer who realizes that things are not going well for his client.

Obligation: Something that someone will do his or her best to avoid fulfilling.

Oblivion: A condition sought by discriminating drinkers of alcoholic beverages.

Obsolete: One-year-old technology.

Obstruct: What a political party can be expected to do when confronted with the plans of a rival party.

Obvious: A subject in which most people are expert.

Occupy: What the military forces do in a country that they have defeated in combat while, at the same time, insisting that they are there as friends.

Office: Men's sanctuary from their family.

Ogle: A natural reaction of men on seeing an attractive female.

Oil: Created over millions of years by decaying fossils, a liquid whose use eventually becomes an addiction to the public.

Olympics: International athletic competition promoted as a friendly competition designed to foster understanding between foreigners which, instead, often produces clashes of cultures leading to hostility between participants and nations.

Ominous: A word used by politicians to gain support for confronting a problem for which they lack the imagination to solve.

Onion: The noblest vegetable of them all, as evidenced by the fact that they are religiously avoided by men out on a date with a woman.

Opera: Musical theater that must be experienced several times before realizing it is even worse than your initial exposure to it.

Opinion: An incorrect viewpoint espoused by someone else.

Optimist: A nearly extinct breed of people who seek the bright side of disaster, even when there is none.

Option: A usually overlooked solution to a problem.

Originality: A lost art.

Oscar: An award given by actors, directors, producers and other motion picture industry personnel during an annual orgy of self-congratulation, which is highlighted by outrageous fashion and often livened by controversial political comments uttered by people who have little, if any, knowledge of the reality of politics.

Outrage: What the public can expect from a politician who finds an opportunity to criticize an opponent.

Oversight: One of the most curious words in the English language. In general usage it is meant to describe an omission. In government it is used to describe a legislative committee empowered to make certain that administrative agencies adhere to ethical and legal standards, something that the latter will seek to avoid at every opportunity.

Oxymoron: A two-word phrase in which the second is not supposed to match the first but in reality does, a few examples being "Good government," "public service," "military intelligence," etc.

P

Paddle: An old-fashioned classroom accessory that the public should demand be re-introduced in the public schools.

Pageant: A competition during which, when they are not cavorting publicly in bathing suits or expensive gowns, attractive young women, who know little of geography, even less of history and nothing of international politics, proclaim that if they are chosen as the winner, will crusade for world peace.

Pamper: What universities do to students who have been given athletic scholarships.

Panama: A make-believe country, which was stolen from Colombia so that international ocean cargo companies could have a shorter trade route between countries of the east and west.

Pander: Something that politicians can be expected to do in order to win or keep support from the voters who elected them to public office.

Panic: A reaction guaranteed to create a crisis where none exists as well as a means of passing responsibility onto someone else during an actual crisis.

Pantomime: The most aggravating form of the performing arts.

Papacy: A high religious office whose chief occupant claims the right to talk to God.

Paperwork: The bread-and-butter of a bureaucrat, who has the power to run the government by using it, ignoring it or losing it..

Parade: A march, usually including musicians, celebrating an event that did not occur the way it is remembered, or the memory of someone whose historic past is scarred by peccadillos that have been kept from the public.

Paranoid: The fate of someone who becomes the head of a nation or a large corporation.

Parasite: A lawyer who has been elected to public office.

Pardon: What criminals can expect from a President of the United States on leaving office as a reward for their past support and future silence.

Parking: Empty space on a street that cities use to extort money from motorists who occupy it with their automobiles.

Party: An event at which people are allowed to make fools of themselves.

Passenger: Someone who puts his or her life in the hands of a pilot of motorist.

Passports: Formal identification papers originally designed to allow people to move freely between countries, but which have since become so bureaucratically regulated that had they existed in 1492, Christopher Columbus would not have bothered to travel across the Atlantic Ocean.

Pathetic: An effort by the Congress of the United States to pass meaningful legislation.

Patience: An attribute endowed to those persons who insist on getting their own way.

Peacekeeper: The worst possible assignment for a soldier.

Peasant: The only class of person who can be trusted.

Pedestrian: A target of wishful thought for motorists.

Peephole: Live television for perverts.

Penalty: An infraction of the rules of American football committed by a player who almost always publicly denies what he knows is his guilt in an effort to convince his fans, teammates and coaches that he is worth every dollar of what he is being overpaid.

Penance: Something demanded of someone who has sinned in the belief that fifteen minutes of repetitive prayer will absolve the miscreant of guilt for even the most heinous crime.

Penny: The smallest monetary unit of the United States coinage, which has been made so anachronistic by inflation that it has become all but worthless, yet remains in circulation because the nation's elected officials are too cowardly to abolish it.

Pension: Government and corporate programs into which people contribute money that they need when they are young in the mistaken belief that their investment will provide them with financial security in their old age.

Pentagon: A large building near Washington, D.C., in which lunatics are employed.

Perfection: An illusion pursued by the naive.

Perjury: Truth, as perceived by members of a jury.

Permanent: What the politicians in the United States Senate and House of Representatives are eager to say they will make of popular legislation, while being fully aware that it cannot be done because one Congress cannot bind a future Congress from making changes to laws.

Permit: Obtained through an aggravating process, a piece of paper that allows homeowners to make the simplest of improvements to their residences only after paying a fee to a municipal government, which then will add the value of the work to the taxable base of the property.

Persecution: What the weak can expect from the strong.

Perverse: Government.

Pet: A domestic animal that should be entrusted only to people who would consider them family members rather than property.

Petition: A system of redress sought by a group that has been organized by an advocate who will think nothing of obtaining fraudulent signatures in order to convince whatever authority is being petitioned that he has wide public support for an issue that ultimately will be forgotten.

Philanthropist: A wealthy person who donates large amounts of money to what appear to be worthy causes, near the end of a calendar year, enabling he or she to deduct the contributions from income that otherwise would be taxed.

Philosopher: Someone unfit for employment in a useful job.

Pharmacy: A candy store for drug addicts.

Phoenix: A giant Arizona suburb that calls itself a city while lacking the downtown that defines cities.

Piety: An addiction to prayer.

Pigeon: A bird that apparently is born straight into adulthood because no one seems to recall ever having seen a baby pigeon.

Pillage: What soldiers of a victorious army claim as their right.

Pipe: A smoking device that men use with occasional nods of their head as a combined and effective means of making them appear intelligent in a group conversation in which they do not have to voice an opinion.

Placebo: Medication for hypochondriacs.

Plan: Something guaranteed to go awry when being implemented because of the failure of its designers to take everything into account.

Plastic: A material used by industry to cut production costs, increase profits and cheapen the consumer's resale value of the finished products containing it.

Plate: A device to extract money from the faithful at a religious gathering.

Platonic: A relationship that men and women like to pretend that they can have with each other.

Pledge: A promise made, usually under financial duress, that later is regretted by all parties concerned.

Plumbing: The greatest of inventions indoors, the worst outdoors.

Poetry: An unnatural way of writing and speaking.

Poker: A card game that is a mix of luck and skill, the latter of which can be decisive if one of the players has mastered the fine art of dealing.

Point: What politicians fail to make when asked a question.

Politician: A con artist who was a failure in a previous career as a burglar.

Pollution: Society's price for prosperity.

Pornography: A lifeline for internet junkies.

Portrait: A picture painted by an artist who can illustrate the flaws in a face that elude a photograph taken by a camera.

Posture: A physical position that mothers encourage on children to avoid a hunchbacked future that almost never occurs except to elderly people who took the advice when they were younger.

Pothole: A feature of road construction that contractors include as extras at no additional cost to the public.

Potpourri: Expensive scented confetti favored by women to the bewilderment of men.

Poverty: An economic condition that only people of means term "is no disgrace."

Power: Authority without accountability.

President: A popularly chosen leader destined to become the most unpopular person in the land.

Prayer: The ultimate ego trip.

Prestige: A 17th Century word that once meant "illusion," which should be explanation enough for the lack of it in the 21st Century.

Pride: Something that every writer eventually surrenders on paper.

Privacy: A fundamental individual right that governments seek to abolish.

Probability: An inexact science ignored by people who enjoy wagering their money.

Procrastination: For most people, a fundamental right.

Profit: Something that oil companies have perfected into an art.

Progress: The replacement of classical beauty with modern ugliness.

Promise: A vow made in haste by people who usually try to avoid keeping it by pretending they had forgotten ever making it.

Promotion: Upper management's method of ridding itself of a lower management problem.

Prompt: Something that should not be expected when awaiting a reply from someone in government.

Proofreader: A field of employment in which there is a serious shortage.

Propaganda: Something governments use in their attempts to retain power.

Property: Anything that humans can claim ownership to, even the skies.

Prophecy: The musings of homeless people believed to be visionaries.

Prosecutor: A government lawyer whose goal is to seek the conviction of an accused person even when the facts indicate innocence.

Provocation: What one government will publicly declare has been committed by another that it is about to attack militarily.

Pseudonym: A false name used by a writer who is embarrassed to admit to authorship.

Psychiatry: An expensive service that allows you to recite a monologue for the entertainment of an audience of one.

Psychology: A profession practiced by persons who could not meet the qualifications required for a license to practice psychiatry.

Pub: In America, a fancy name intended to add prestige to a bar or tavern.

Public: The harshest of all critics.

Publicist: A person whose career is based on deceit.

Publicity: Something politicians eagerly seek when running for office, but just as eagerly try to avoid after they are elected.

Pump: A mechanical device which, when attached to a gasoline station meter, has an appetite even more voracious than a casino slot machine.

Pundit: A political analyst or columnist who is considered brilliant when he or she guesses correctly at least once during his or her career.

Puppet: A form of government in which a weak country's international strings are pulled by a stronger one in return for monetary and political assistance on which the former has become dependent.

Purpose: Hidden behind ideals, an excuse for doing something that often is harmful to others.

Q

Quack: What patients hear when their medical condition is being explained to them by physicians.

Quagmire: Something everyone is fated to stumble into at least once in their lifetime.

Quaint: What people who believe that they are sophisticated think of something that they never would enjoy experiencing.

Quality: Mass production and profit has eliminated this word from use in the description of manufactured products.

Quarry: Land legally turned into an eyesore for the profit of a company at the expense of the health of its workers.

Question: A written or oral request that rarely receives the answer it seeks.

Quiche: Something that men will reluctantly eat only in the company of women in order to impress a false appreciation of sensitivity on the fairer sex.

Quiet: The preferred company of the duo that includes "peace."

Quintuplets: The worst nightmare of parenthood.

Quiz: A question-and-answer game designed to give contestants an opportunity to impress others with their knowledge, but more often exposes their lack of it.

Quorum: The most difficult thing to achieve on the floor of either the United States Senate or House of Representatives.

Quota: Unreal goals that executives and managers set for workers.

Quote: Something that someone purportedly has told to a news reporter which, after it has been made public, is denied by the original source if he or she finds it to be embarrassing.

R

Racism: An extreme form of ostracism once widely practiced, sometimes accompanied by violence, by persons of one race or ethnic group against persons of another and so pervasive that it required passage of equality laws to force people into behaving the way they should have in the first place without the threat of legal action.

Radical: What anyone who wants to change the established order is labeled by those who are content with things just the way they are.

Radio: A forum for talk show hosts whose only talent is shouting, especially when a guest or caller offers an opinion backed by facts that differs from the position of the host.

Rain: Weather that brings relief from the boredom of sunshine.

Raise: The only legislation that lawmakers can be expected to approve when applied to their salaries.

Random: An event or incident likely to upset the most carefully designed plans.

Ransack: What law enforcement officers will do to your home should they ever enter it with a search warrant.

Rationale: Fraud in disguise.

Rattle: A warning device that evolution would have been better served had it attached it to a human rather than to a snake.

Reality: Something that most people try to avoid.

Realization: Awareness that usually arrives too late.

Reason: Accountability without the excuse.

Reassurance: The first indication that an employee receives that his job is not in jeopardy when, in fact, it is.

Recipe: Instructions for the creation of something to eat, which usually turns out to be unpalatable on the cook's first attempt.

Recipient: A person who receives something unwanted.

Recommendation: Advice destined to be ignored when issued by a government-appointed commission.

Reconnaissance: Internationally sanctioned espionage when performed by uniformed military personnel.

Recruit: A method of filling available positions in the public and private sectors, including the military, by which propaganda specialists make promises to prospective employees that are unlikely to be kept.

Redundant: Television news and political speeches.

Reference: The dubious recommendation of an employer fearful of refusing to endorse an employee who had been fired for incompetence because of the possibility that the latter might sue for slander.

Reform: A movement aimed at making bad things worse.

Refrigerator: A storage box that ruins the taste of most foods and beverages.

Refund: Something often promised but rarely given.

Regret: An annoying prodding by the conscience that should be ignored unless amends can be made for whatever wrong has been committed.

Regulations: Rules devised by bureaucrats to justify their jobs.

Reinforcements: When called for by a military commander, an indication that disaster is imminent.

Relatives: Jurors always ready to sit in judgment of each other.

Relaxation: Exercise for the thinking person.

Religion: Mindless belief.

Reluctance: Something everyone should be stricken with when asked to volunteer.

Remote: Once a place where a person could relax, now an annoying device used by the person with whom you are watching television.

Rendezvous: A meeting of two persons that will end in harm either for the participants or an innocent third party.

Replacement: A poor substitute for something original.

Reptile: A lawyer who specializes in divorce or personal injury cases.

Rescue: Attempts to save people from the harm they do to themselves because of foolish behavior during severe weather in mountainous areas.

Research: Legal plagiarism.

Reservation: Once a large area of land given to Native Americans where a government was eager for them to live in isolation, but now, thanks to the federal courts, a smaller place where they build casinos that allow descendants of settlers from Europe and other continents to pay reparations through gambling losses.

Resignation: A face-saving word used by an executive who has been fired from his job.

Resort: An artificial holiday destination.

Respect: Something that never should be granted to authority.

Responsibility: Acceptance of the blame for something that goes wrong, something that people will go to extremes to avoid doing.

Restaurant: A place where young people who have been raised on home cooking discover that food can taste good.

Result: Something looked forward to until it occurs.

Retaliation: Revenge on a grand scale.

Retirement: A time of life when people are led to believe that they can finally relax in the comfort of their homes, only to discover that they spend more time working there than they did while in the service of an employer.

Reunion: A gathering of friends or family members who have not seen each other in a long time, the result of which is a resolve by the attendees never to gather again.

Revenge: The worst reason for doing anything.

Revision: What happens to recorded history when a political party takes control of a government and decides to put its own spin on the past.

Revolution: An event aimed at cleansing society of its ills which, in the process, creates a new set of ills that only can be cured by another revolution.

Reward: The highest form of bribery.

Rights: Something immediately demanded by someone who has broken the law.

Rock: Discordant music performed by entertainers who cover their inability to sing by shouting to the accompaniment of mostly electronic instruments played by people with no appreciation of harmony.

Role: Something that some persons play rarely, while for others it is a part of their daily routine.

Romania: An Eastern European country that has managed to escape consignment to obscurity because of its association with the legend of vampires, including the fictional Count Dracula.

Romans: If you understood the Monty Python movie, you'll know that these were the people who gave the world roads, public safety, education, public water and wine.

Rout: The usual outcome of what begins as a retreat.

Routine: What people can expect of the day upon awakening in the morning.

Rule: Instruction awaiting an opportunity to be applied.

Rumor: Something to be spread.

Rustic: The polite term for shabby.

S

Sabotage: The specialty of a self-proclaimed freedom fighter.

Sacrilege: Something committed often by even the most religiously devout.

Sage: A status achieved by men who reach the age of 80 years while managing to avoid being diagnosed as senile.

Saint: A dead sinner.

Safety: A condition, usually attached to a specific place, where the unwary erroneously believe that can find immunity from disaster.

Sale: A retail slogan designed to entice wives to buy something they do not need at a price lower than what they would have normally paid so that they can later brag to their husbands about how much money they saved.

Saloon: The poor man's pub.

Sanctions: Ineffective political and economic pressure brought to bear on countries in an effort to convince them to change their ways.

Sarcasm: The art of the arrogant.

Satan: God with a sense of humor.

Sauce: A thick liquid concoction designed to ruin the simple taste of good food.

Sauna: A hellish device designed for maximum discomfort.

Sausage: A meat product that often contains more grain than meat.

Savings: A financial anachronism in a consumer-driven society.

Scandal: Deserved public embarrassment of someone who has had an ethical or moral lapse to the enjoyment of others, especially those who have been able to keep their peccadilloes from exposure.

Scarf: Winter survival gear in Scandinavia.

Scheme: A government program that pours huge amounts of taxpayer money into a project that promises to enrich the lives of the public, most of which did not support it in the first place and whose only satisfaction will be to joint the chant of "I told you so" when the program proves a wasteful failure.

Scholar: Someone too intelligent to be a teacher.

School: A place where teachers tell lies to children.

Scone: An English cake baked so dry that only the addition of jam, preserves or cream can make it palatable.

Scoundrel: A sociable criminal.

Scruples: A quality claimed by people who pretend to have principles.

Second: In competition, the highest ranking achieved by a loser.

Secret: Something that retains its status when known by only one person.

Secretary: A person who does most of the work for which his or her immediate superior gets all of the credit.

Security: Governmental responsibility, usually implemented at the cost of freedom.

Sedative: Medication that should be considered being added to the public water supply of nations that go on patriotic rampages.

Seminary: Boot camp for aspiring pedophiles.

Senior: Someone who believes that the public owes him or her a living.

Sensible: A quality lacking in most people.

Sensitivity: A mask worn by people in an emotionally misguided effort to conceal the truth from others.

Sequel: A second-rate novel or motion picture that picks up where a successful earlier version of the same story left off.

Sermon: A political speech designed to win votes for God.

Servant: A well-mannered employee of an ill-mannered employer.

Service: Something that once was a routine part of consumer commerce, but now is rarely available and no longer expected.

Seventy: An age at which agnostics and atheists begin to rediscover religion, and at which conservatives begin to acquire an appreciation for liberalism.

Shakespeare: A 16th Century playwright whose works have remained so popular that the mere mention of one of his plays coming to town is guaranteed to fill the theater with spectators, who wish they could be elsewhere and have no idea what they are watching, but want to be able to make friends and neighbors believe that they have an appreciation for artistic culture.

Shareholders: Victims of legalized thievery.

Shelf: Reserved seating for the results of government studies.

Shill: A salesperson, advertising executive or public relations specialist.

Shopping: Boredom for a male accompanying a female, as evidenced on the faces of the former as they wander from one store to another.

Shower: An invention of the devil, designed to deny humans of pleasure.

Showgirl: An aspiring actress whose talent lies anywhere but on the stage.

Shrink: The art of reproducing something in a smaller size, which the Japanese have perfected while, at the same time, improving quality.

Shyness: A disguise used by people with a desire for greatness.

Shyster: An apt title for an attorney because it has been adapted from the name "Scheuster," a lawyer of the 19th Century whose professional practices were considered questionable.

Sieve: A place where government secrets make their debut.

Sigh: An attention-getting device used by people to express boredom or displeasure.

Silence: The only thing left that politicians have not been able to exploit.

Simplicity: The most workable idea, which usually is arrived at with only the most difficult and complex thought process.

Sin: Organized religion's definition of fun.

Singer: In 21st Century terminology, a person who shouts as quickly as he or she does loudly so that listeners cannot understand the words.

Siphon: The art of acquiring free gasoline.

Skeptic: A cynic who refuses to commit to his or her principles.

Sleep: Practice for death.

Slipper: The only footwear that men feel comfortable wearing.

Slob: An unmarried male.

Slogan: A cleverly worded, but cheap and tawdry, phrase used in political campaigns by candidates who have little of substance to say.

Slum: A gold mine for landlords.

Slush: Melting snow that holds surprises for people who are unfamiliar with the potential hazards of life in a big city.

Smoking: Suicide on the installment plan.

Snag: An unseen feature built into every venture.

Snake: An animal whose reputation has been maligned by its unfortunate portrayal in the Old Testament of the Bible. Would the dog have suffered a similar fate had it been the culprit that offered Eve the apple?.

Snollygoster: An antiquated word that sent news reporters scrambling to learn its meaning in the 1950's after President Harry Truman used it to describe Senator Joseph McCarthy, only to discover that it might have two definitions. One, found in old dictionaries, explains that it is an "unscrupulous politician." The other, later acknowledged by Truman, is that it also was another word for "bastard."

Snoop: A neighbor.

Snow: Admired by people as one of nature's beauties until it comes time to shovel it.

Sobriety: A condition in which everything looks hopeless.

Soccer: An international sport that fans keep predicting will become widely popular in the United States, while ignoring the reality that few Americans appreciate watching 22 men kick a ball around the field for 90 minutes without scoring more than one or two points.

Socialist: Someone who believes that the government knows best and tries to implement their ideas when elected to public office, only to be replaced by a conservative who promises less government while quietly increasing the size of the bureaucracy.

Society: A group of people who have banded together for protection before turning against each other.

Sociology: A murky neo-science devoted to finding solutions that do not work for problems that do not exist.

Sociopath: Someone who seeks the highest political office in the land.

Software: Computer programs rushed to the market by companies with little regard for errors, leaving the product's faults to be corrected by customers who have paid high prices to be among the first to possess them.

Solitude: A state not available to someone with more than one relative or friend.

Song: Words strung together in sentences to the accompaniment of music, sometimes objectionable, often ridiculous, that no one would dare use in polite conversation.

Sophisticated: An affliction of the pretentious.

Source: A person, sometimes real, often imaginary, favored by journalists hungry for notoriety.

Souvenirs: Items purchased by tourists who do not recognize them for the junk that they are until after they arrive home.

Specialist: Someone clever enough to get a job that requires little work.

Spectacle: Something that political leaders who lead long enough will make of themselves.

Speculation: The last resort of a journalist in need of a story.

Speech: A lengthy boring monologue designed to put its listeners to sleep before they can think of asking the speaker embarrassing questions.

Speed: Something that possesses drivers when they get their first motor vehicle.

Spelling: An educational discipline no longer taught in the schools, as evidenced by the works of communications professionals.

Spending: A game at which women always can beat men.

Sponsor: Someone who is strong-armed to provide financial support for an event that promises little return for the investment.

Sports: Athletic competitions in which pampered professionals are allowed to circumvent the rules by intimidation of everyone else for the benefit of manufacturers of steroids and other performance-enhancement substances.

Sportsmanship: An antiquated form of behavior, usually associated with sports, that became extinct in the late 20th Century.

Spy: Someone willing to sell out anything and anyone for money or dedication to a dubious cause.

Stability: A state that has eluded civilization in 5,000 years of recorded history.

Stage: If, as Shakespeare claimed "all the world" is one, then it begs the question to sit of where the audience is supposed to sit.

Stands: An oddly named section of a stadium where spectators sit instead of being upright on two feet.

Starlet: An attractive young woman whose acting career will be limited to playing minor roles in major films until she begins taking major roles in insignificant films before ultimately moving on to waiting tables in restaurants.

Start: A keyboard button that takes users to a place where they can turn off, rather than start, their computers.

Starvation: The result of a protest known as a hunger strike, during which people believe that they can hurt someone else by not eating.

Statement: A public pronouncement issued on behalf of a public official or candidate for political office who is too fearful of appearing in person to explain why he or she said or did something embarrassing.

Statesman: A politician who outlives his failures.

Statistics: Numbers that are manipulated for gain, usually by charitable organizations in search of financial donations,

Stench: An obnoxious odor resulting from government legislation concocted behind closed doors.

Sting: A sanctioned law enforcement activity in which people are secretly induced into performing criminal acts that they might not otherwise commit.

Stress: A hereditary disease that children pass on to their parents.

Stuff: Material things accumulated by women.

Stylish: Something that men cannot be accused of being.

Suburb: A boring artificial community where people can watch television and sleep without having to endure the vitality of cities, the friendship of towns and the natural beauty of the countryside.

Subsidy: Public financing of private industry for the benefit of corporate executives.

Subtitles: Words added in the form of text to the bottom of foreign language motion picture scenes, in the belief that they will allow English-speaking movie-goers to understand what is being spoken by the filmed actors when, in reality, most of the people in such audiences cannot read fast enough to digest the dialogue.

Subtlety: Something that eludes most people.

Subversive: A patriot who dares to publicly disagree with the conduct of his government in times of war.

Success: An accident of persistent failure.

Sugar: The lifeblood of the dental profession.

Sun: Worshiped by pagans for centuries, it may be the most sensible of gods not only because it sustains life, but also because it is visible.

Superficial: Television news.

Supermarket: A large one-stop store that has all but killed off independent butchers, bakeries and greengrocers in the United States, insuring the destruction of the quality of food and the ruination of American taste buds.

Superstition: The foundation of religion.

Support: Something waiting to be yanked out from under at the most critical of moments.

T

Tattoo: Expensive body art usually acquired by young people who, when older, wish they could bear the pain and afford the cost of having it removed.

Taboo: An old-fashioned notion that has become obsolete in the 21st Century.

Tarot: A deck of cards depicting colorful medieval-style images that is used by charlatans to extract money from the gullible.

Tawdry: Government behavior without public disclosure.

Taxes: Money taken from workers who have earned it to pay government officials whose job it is to find new ways to extract more money from their victims.

Teacher: An overpaid bureaucrat who has become so dependent on semi-accurate printed material that he or she becomes unaware of the lies and half-truths being taught to children in classrooms.

Tears: A biological trick used by women to end arguments that they realize they cannot win.

Technology: An invention or scientific advancement that is defective when first marketed to the public, which pays millions of dollars to test it for flaws, then later purchases the improved version only to find that, within a year or two, it has become obsolete.

Teenager: A resident of a world that adults never see.

Teleconference: An impersonal meeting of people connected to each other from the perceived safety of locations so distant that the participants rarely are able to discern their professional peril until it is too late.

Telephone: A device that, in the 21st Century has become government's silent entry into the homes of people.

Television: The lowest form of art, which explains its popularity.

Temperance: Perhaps the most peculiar of diseases because not only does it afflict persons with a distaste for alcohol, but it also instills its victims with a desire to pass the illness on to others.

Template: A design concept for the lazy.

Temptation: Under the right circumstances, something into which everyone is willing to be led.

Tennessee: The last refuge for a moonshiner.

Terror: A fear of someone or something that can do great harm to others, on which a war declared by the United States and other nations cannot be won due to a misinterpretation of the enemy by American politicians and media. Instead of trying to fight "terror," which probably never can be eliminated, they should be going after the real enemy – "terrorism."

Textbooks: Classroom materials that often are unreliable because errors committed in the research and publication of material in previous editions are repeated in subsequent volumes by writers and editors who are too lazy to check for accuracy and by publishers who set unrealistic deadlines.

Thanksgiving: A traditional American family feast honoring the first such meal at which Native Americans are traditionally absent.

That: A word used by women to describe something specific to men.

Theory: Self-congratulatory guesswork.

Thesis: A document lacking original or practical thought that entitles a university student to an academic degree, sometimes with high honors.

Thief: Someone who values property so much that he must acquire it by any means possible.

Terse: A quality that lacking in most politicians and writers.

Threat: The first word applied by a chief of state to describe another nation on which he or she intends to declare war.

Three: A number believed by many people to have mystical properties of repetition, as suggested in phrases such as – "Three on a match," "Three is a crowd," "Three strikes and out." Other examples are found in religion – the Holy Trinity, Peter denying Christ three times, Christ being one of three men crucified on the same day. Some people even believe that everything bad happens in threes. For instance, when two celebrities die, believers will announce that another death will follow, which they will link to the first two even though the third may occur weeks or months later.

Time: Something that no one seems to have enough of, especially the elderly.

Timeshare: A real estate concept in which people invest money that allows them the right to occupy a housing unit in a resort for one or more weeks a year, only to later learn that they have invested in nothing and can retrieve only a fraction of their original investment should they attempt to sell.

Toadstool: Something that should encourage people to think at least twice before embarking on a hunt for wild mushrooms.

Toast: Slices of bread, from which some of the questionable nutrition has been removed by burning its surface, that get the English to drop their natural reserve and, instead, become excited over the prospect of coating it with jam and eating it accompanied by tea.

Tobacco: An instrument of Native American revenge for the crimes committed upon them by generations of white European settlers and their descendants.

Today: A period of 24 hours during which people look forward toward its end with the hope that the next 24-hour period will be a better day.

Tofu: Make-believe food

Toilet: A word that has become all but taboo in an America that has become obsessed with renaming anything that seems even mildly unsightly. Its latest incarnation of "rest room" can be misleading to foreigners truly in need only of a rest

Tolerance: Indifference in disguise.

Tomato: A vegetable (sometimes considered a fruit) that Italians believe is manufactured from cardboard in the United States.

Tombstone: A permanent address marker in a neighborhood never visited by the postman.

Tomorrow: The 24-hour period, which people look forward to being better than the previous day only to learn that, not only is it rarely better, but often worse.

Tongue: The most overused part of the human anatomy.

Torture: Watching golf on television.

Tour: A form of travel during which people are rushed from one place to another, allowing them to look without seeing, eat without dining and listen without learning, all at a price they are led to believe is a bargain, proving the adage that you "get what you pay for."

Town: A place that suffers from an inferiority complex because it lacks the vibrant life of a big city and the picture postcard atmosphere of a village.

Tradition: Institutionalized laziness.

Tragedy: When women become like their mothers.

Transcript: A printed record of government proceedings, with the embarrassing parts edited for public consumption.

Transfer: A soldier's request that is not likely to occur.

Translation: The conversion of words in one language to another, guaranteeing that at least part of the original intent will be lost.

Transvestite: The ultimate arbiter of fashionable wear.

Travel: A search for the fantasy of something better.

Treaty: An agreement between governments waiting for the appropriate moment to break it.

Treason: Refusal to speak out publicly against the policies of a national leader in time of war.

Trekkie: Someone in dire need of getting a life, but prevented from doing so by an addiction to a decades-old science fiction cult television series.

Trial: An event where justice often is miscarried.

Trick: The part of "trick or treat" that appeals to teenagers on Halloween.

Trifle: A problem of importance to the younger generation that has no interest to the older generation.

Trivia: Information considered unimportant by those who lack knowledge of it.

Trouble: The most interesting of possibilities for a thinking person.

Truant: A student with a sense of adventure.

Trust: Something that never should be granted to politicians.

Truth: Something that has different meanings to different people.

Tuition: Outrageous fees charged to students by institutions of higher learning in order to finance non-academic pursuits.

Turbulence: One of the free extras of airline travel.

Turkey: A bird which was named by Americans for a country where no such bird existed simply because it was the fashion of the times to name any new food after the seat of the Ottoman Empire.

Typewriter: An antique word processor with class.

U

Ultimate: The highest possible achievement, usually proclaimed by manufacturers of products that will remain at the top until something better comes along.

Underdog: A person or team that is not expected to win an athletic event, but enjoys the role of spoiler until it is time to play, when the result usually validates its designation.

Understanding: An agreement in principle between opposing sides that have secretly decided to stand firm on their original viewpoints.

Unisex: Public toilet facilities, courtesy of the women's rights movement.

Universal: A word used by people to describe something of wide appeal to or acceptance by humans, while arrogantly ignoring that it might not be favored by other beings that probably exist elsewhere in a universe populated by billions of galaxies.

Unknown: The residue of discovery.

Unlikely: What the seller of something tells to a buyer in lieu of a guarantee to ease the latter's concerns over whether a product may not perform as advertised.

Unwitting: A condition that instills enthusiasm in people who have been convinced to invest their financial assets into a get-rich-quick scheme.

Unworthy: What a politician will say of himself with false humility, but only after he has been elected to public office.

Uproar: Public support for demagoguery.

V

Vampire: From the antiquated word "vamp," a woman with so voracious an appetite for money that she can suck the numbers off a man's credit card.

Variable: Something unexpected, waiting for the wrong moment to appear.

Vermin: Politicians whose dining habits are limited to nibbling at the edges of constitutional rights.

Vice: Amusement in its highest form.

Victim: Everyone, at least once in their lifetime.

Victory: What generals claim when they have conducted a successful retreat from a battle that they have lost.

Vietnam: A small Asian country where France was taught, and has remembered, painful political and military lessons in the 1950's while the United States, which learned similar lessons there in the 1960's and 1970's, appears to have since forgotten.

Village: Picture postcard atmosphere aside, a place that is boring to anyone who does not enjoy antique shops and tea rooms.

Violence: One of the normal conditions of humans.

Virginia: A place where progress never is allowed to stand in the path of tradition.

Virtue: A mask that comes with the uniform worn by clerics.

Virus: A microscopic form of life that once was feared for the dangers it presented to human health but which, in the 21st Century, has mutated into a form feared more for what it can do to a computer.

Visionary: A person who dreams of a future without thinking of the possibility of it becoming a nightmare for others.

Volunteer: Someone who is coerced into doing something that he or she normally would not attempt and which stronger-willed and more intelligent people will not attempt.

Vote: A means of public political expression designed to deceive people who live in democracies into believing that their opinions matter.

Voyeur: The most discriminating of spectators.

Vulgarity: A form of speech guaranteed to add life to an otherwise boring gathering.

Vulnerability: A condition that can strike anyone, usually at the most inopportune moments.

W

Wager: A step on the road to poverty.

Wages: A sum of money paid to a worker who believes he has been paid too little by an employer who believes he has paid too much.

Waiting: What a young man can expect to do when he arrives at the appointed time for a date with a young woman.

War: A natural condition of civilization interrupted by periods of an artificial process known as peace.

Warning: An implied threat made in an effort by someone who has no intention of acting on it in an effort to dissuade someone else from doing what they want.

Warranty: A guarantee that consumers believe insures the workings of a manufactured product until they discover the word "limited" in the fine print.

Washington: The capital of the United States, whose buildings appear obsessed with trying very hard to look like the monuments of ancient Greece.

Water: An environment used by fish to fornicate.

Waver: The temporary hesitation of sensible people.

We: A word sports fans use when describing their favorite team, even though their only interest in it may be from afar.

Wealth: The path to poor health.

Weapons: Devices designed to kill people and destroy property, but described as necessary for peaceful purposes by nations seeking those more deadly than their neighbors possess.

Weather: Nature's appreciation for the absurd.

Web: Once a trap woven by spiders to catch unwary flies, now refined by humans into an electronic trap to catch unwary persons.

Weeds: The only plants guaranteed to grow in a garden.

Weekdays: A period during which people can take a break from the tyranny of religion, except for the relentless pursuit of Jehovah's Witnesses.

Weird: What people who believe that they should not act on inner feelings that friends and relatives would not understand call people who are not afraid of doing so.

West: A direction that Horace Greeley once advised be taken by a young man in search of a future. While hailed by people who followed the New York journalist's advice, it should be noted that Greeley stayed put in the east.

Will: The last expression of a person's sense of humor.

Window: A glass-covered opening in a building used by people inside to spy on people outside.

Wine: A pleasant alcoholic beverage that the United States government, in its infinite wisdom, has corrupted by requiring producers to adulterate it with sulfites, thereby lending credence to the claims of the French that California wine is really fruit punch in disguise.

Wisdom: A quality believed to be endowed to an older person who inevitably will reveal a lack of it by speaking.

Witness: Someone whose recollection of something is bound to differ from the recollections of others.

WMD: A sort of acronym meaning "Weapons of Mass Destruction," concocted in the White House to help gain public support for the Gulf War of 1991 because it was considered more ominous than the old term "special weapons." It has since been so overused by politicians and the media to the point of annoyance that it is destined to be changed to something more frightening in the future.

Words: Letters strung together to form what must be pleasing to the taste buds considering how often people eat them.

Women: Human creatures who live longer than men because, unlike men, they do not live with women.

Work: A lost ethic.

World: The first half of the title that Americans enjoy awarding to the winners of athletic events that are conducted only in the United States.

Worsen: What will happen to a bad situation before it improves.

Wrestling: Acrobatic play acting promoted as a competitive sport.

Writer: Someone who claims that filling paper with words is hard work.

X, Y, Z

Xmas: The word that took "Christ" out of Christmas.

X-rated: A label that once was attached to movies that now are R-rated.

Yardage: Territory violently sought by overgrown athletes on an American football field.

Yawn: A recommended method for breaking up a dull gathering.

Yes: A word often used by people who really mean to say "no."

Yesterday: Twenty-four, usually misspent, hours that you'll never see again.

Yoga: A form of mental exercise that does not require thinking.

Yogurt: Inedible fermented bacteria.

Youth: An age class of people denounced by their elders.

Yugoslavia: A perfectly sensible country that was dismantled in the late 20th Century with the help of the countries of the democratic west, leading to the creation of splinter republics, one of which adopted the worst name of any nation in history – the Former Yugoslav Republic of Macedonia.

Zen: Relaxation in the guise of religion.

Zest: A stimulating experience that disappears with the first encounter with reality.

Zombie: What a person becomes by staying in the same job for too long.

Zoo: A prison for animals serving life sentences for the crime of existence.

THE END (The ultimate destination of everything)